DREAM STATE

DREAM STATE

california
in the movies

MICK LaSALLE

H

Heyday, Berkeley, California

Library of Congress Cataloging-in-Publication Data

Names: LaSalle, Mick, author.
Title: Dream state : California in the movies / Mick LaSalle.
Description: Berkeley : Heyday, [2021] | Includes index.
Identifiers: LCCN 2020045993 | ISBN 9781597145312 (hardcover) | ISBN 9781597145329 (epub)
Subjects: LCSH: California--In motion pictures. | Place (Philosophy) in motion pictures.
Classification: LCC PN1995.9.C325 L37 2021 | DDC 791.4309794--dc23
LC record available at https://lccn.loc.gov/2020045993

Cover Design: Archie Ferguson
Interior Design/Typesetting: Ashley Ingram

Published by Heyday
P.O. Box 9145, Berkeley, California 94709
(510) 549-3564
heydaybooks.com

Printed in East Peoria, Illinois, by Versa Press, Inc.

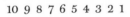

For Jennifer Hengen and in memory of Bob Graham.

They got me here.

CONTENTS

INTRODUCTION

The dream is always in sight and always out of reach. California as a state of being is aspirational, envious, driving toward something, often literally, always figuratively, and, in some fundamental way, never, ever getting there.

The tourists that walk along San Francisco's Marina Green, with the sailboats to their right and the Golden Gate Bridge in front of them, think to themselves, if only . . . If only I lived here I could get to that thing, that inner place I've always wanted, that full arrival, that mix of assured achievement and complete relaxation, that feeling of purpose and victory, that balance of adventure and civilization, where you are always there at the center of things and always thriving, and everywhere you look there's splendor.

Likewise, the tourists in their rental cars, driving down Wilshire or Sunset or Santa Monica Boulevard, with music playing out of four speakers, and the warm breeze blowing, and the palm trees climbing and climbing into the sky for one small burst of life . . . they know it, too. It's the California feeling, Los Angeles version. It's the Randy Newman "I Love L.A." feeling, of being unstoppable and brilliant, a glamorous big shot that can do all things and is part of the moment.

Many of those tourists having these feelings and sensations will, in only a matter of days, find themselves staring out the window of an airplane, taking a last look at the place, as the bridges turn into toys and the mountains into rocks, and they will feel like they've been ejected out of paradise. But what they won't know is that the feeling that they had and will carry with them—of seeing it and wanting it and not quite grasping it—is how the natives often feel, too.

California is a place that breeds both spiritual satisfaction and spiritual envy. Most big cities in America feel like a challenge. They look hard, and they are indeed as hard as they look. But California's big cities create an illusion of tranquility and loveliness, so that if you're in one of those cities and your life is anything but tranquil or lovely, glorious or triumphant, it feels like something is a little off. Obviously, there's a party going on. Obviously, you deserve to be invited. And obviously you just can't locate the address. So *obviously* something is very wrong, but not with you—no, never with you—and not even with the city or state. The problem is the universe in general.

THIS IS A BOOK ABOUT CALIFORNIA IN THE MOVIES, but it's not a history of the film business in California, because that would come close to being a general history of American movies. Nor is it a chronicle of every time California has ever been mentioned or depicted on screen. The abridged version of that would run a good thousand pages. Rather, this is a book about two things, about the idea of California as depicted in movies, and about California ideas that have made their way into the culture, through movies.

These ideas, often subliminal, often unconscious, presented through a succession of arresting images, huge emotions, and beautiful places and people, have had a powerful impact on Americans' sense of themselves and on the world's sense of America. These ideas suggest values and a vision of life, and while this California vision can't be completely defined or encapsulated, a general summary is possible.

The California vision is, first of all, one of material splendor. It is a vision of glamour. It is often a vision of youth or of youthfulness. But it suggests more than material things. It suggests an environment in which individualism can be celebrated, and in which romanticized individuals—our proxies, in the form of movie stars—are iconicized as embodying particular moral values that we can, in turn, aspire to and emulate. This vision feeds a longing so intense that it feels spiritual, in that it promotes the idea of an ideal world in which we can be loved and worthy of love, not for anything we do, but simply for being ourselves.

In a sense, the California vision is the ultimate expression of an idealized capitalism: Hollywood celebrates the individual, not the collective. Indeed, even when it celebrates the collective, it still celebrates the individual. It shows a mass of citizens marching forward to rebuild San Francisco at the end of *San Francisco* (1936), but it shows Clark Gable front and center, practically leading the way.

Hitler's Germany and Stalin's Soviet Union, which both arrived early in the history of the feature film, recognized the power of the medium for disseminating ideas through story, and so they took over the film industry. In the United States, at roughly the same time, censors tried to take over the film industry with a restrictive Production Code that stifled screen content and tried actively to promote traditional values. The censors enjoyed surprising success for a surprisingly long time, but eventually they could no longer hold back the tide of human nature and of movie-influenced morality. The movies' steady drip of glamour, romance, and splendor did its job. Sometimes the ideas that filmmakers don't even know they're expressing are more powerful than the things they consciously intend to say.

Of course, not all movies are set in California or even shot in California, and movies are not a monolith that say the same things all the time. There are movies that present a bleak vision of America, and of California, and we know, from the films that are frequently honored in foreign film festivals, that our European friends in particular gravitate toward the dark side of American life, if only to reassure themselves that they're better off where they are. Half the time, they're right to think so.

But I would maintain that even the bleaker depictions of American life usually celebrate and idealize individual personality and effort. Likewise, in a disguised form, they often celebrate the ideals of youth or youthfulness, glamour, individualism, and the notion that people are worth loving just for being themselves. Even the depiction of bleakness suggests an ideal in the opposite direction, and the very fact that heroes usually *succeed* in American movies at least offers the hope that some kind of California dream is within reach of everyone.

That's the promise on the other side: Sex and glory and

money in your pocket, and everyone loves you, and you're beautiful forever. There are always obstacles in the way, but the movies provide that destination.

I GREW UP IN NEW YORK, and when I first came to California in my mid-twenties, I was very thrown by the people. They were friendly, but they weren't warm. If I went to a restaurant, the hostess might talk to me as if I were her old buddy, but in a way that was *too* familiar, that would be considered rude or just weird in New York. Yet for all their seeming cheer, these Californians were hard to know. I knew how things worked on the East Coast: The people have a hard shell, until they figure out that you're all right. Then the shell goes away, and you know them. On the West Coast, friendliness itself was a form of shell, which I found very disconcerting. It took a while to stop reflexively opening up in response to seeming invitations, only to feel myself observed as if by two eyes peeking through a barricade. It took a long time just to feel I was on solid ground with people.

In time, I came to realize that this odd combination of friendliness and distance was the result of a general dislocation. People come to California from other places. Very often, they come alone. They arrive without family or friends. So they have to talk to the strangers that they meet or else they will lose their minds. They brazen it out, adopt a false bravado, an impervious armor of good cheer. All the same, they can't exactly *trust* anybody, not at first, not for a while. To protect themselves, they accept living with loneliness, and this becomes their way of going through life.

I sometimes wonder if we can see that same wary reserve in the actors that grew up in California. Think of Marilyn Monroe, Robert Redford, Jennifer Aniston, Gloria Grahame, Diane Keaton, Kevin Costner, Jennifer Jason Leigh, Zooey Deschanel, and Kristen Stewart. Aside from being from California, do they have anything in common? Yes, two things: (1) They have an undertone of ruefulness, as if they understand and accept loneliness as an inescapable condition of life, and (2) They have something inside that they're never going to show you. You can watch them forever and you'll never see it. They'll show you *a lot*—they'll show you some really wonderful things—but they'll never do an Al Pacino on you. They will never back up the dump truck and unload. They will never give you everything they've got.

So, yes, that reserve is a California actor thing, too. But then again, there's Tom Hanks (Concord), Jessica Chastain (Sacramento), and Linda Cardellini (Redwood City)—they're pretty warm and unguarded. So maybe that reserve is a *Southern* California thing. Oh, but wait again, what about Drew Barrymore (Culver City), who couldn't be more down to earth? And what about Leonardo DiCaprio (Los Angeles), one of the most wide-open, unbounded actors of his generation?

Clearly, there's no hard-and-fast rule here. When generalizing about something as huge as California, the best you can hope to find are tendencies, which are, let's hope, useful, interesting, and maybe even true.

In any case, the more important point here is that this aspect of California people has its analogue in California itself. The state presents an inviting and reassuring surface, but underneath there's complexity, darkness, and sometimes even threat. It is, frustratingly, as magnificent as it seems, too gorgeous and impressive and life-expanding to ever be dismissed or fled without regret. But it's not easy.

But then, nothing ever is in the Naked City. Or the Emerald City. Or anywhere.

CHAPTER ONE

The Wizard of Oz Is a Movie
about Hollywood

The wizard in *The Wizard of Oz* originally hailed from a quiet, dull place in the Midwest, and yet he ended up in a colorful, beautiful land where the light was lovely and the weather was always nice. Once in this new place, he did what any self-respecting megalomaniac might do: He decided that he should be boss. He tricked the credulous people of Oz by claiming to be all-powerful, and by becoming a phony on a grand scale, he got to live in a palace.

Now it's years later. Dorothy and her three friends arrive in Oz, and they go straight to the wizard's palace, hoping he will grant them favors. He agrees, but on one condition. In L. Frank Baum's original book (1900), the condition is that they kill the Wicked Witch of the West. In the movie, the condition is that they bring back the witch's broom, which amounts to the same thing but has the advantage of sounding softer and providing a visual—always good in a movie.

We must assume the wizard has done this before. We don't know this for sure, but it stands to reason. The man has no power.

He can't grant anyone a favor because he can't *do* anything. Yet his subjects will keep coming to him, begging. His solution: When people ask him to do something difficult, he just tells them to go kill the one person all but guaranteed to kill *them*, i.e., the witch. The wizard, though he later claims to be "a very good man . . . just a very bad wizard," is just not a nice guy.

Of course, as we all remember, Dorothy melts the witch and she and her three companions return to Oz's palace to claim their prizes. That's when the wizard is revealed as a fraud. What can he do then? In the book, he gives them each a phony version of the thing they want—fake versions of a brain and a heart for the Scarecrow and Tin Man, respectively, and a bogus courage potion for the Cowardly Lion. He counts on them being stupid enough or generous enough to settle for little.

In the movie, however, he does something subtly more interesting. He can't give the Cowardly Lion courage, so he gives him a medal. He can't give the Scarecrow a brain, so he gives him a degree. He can't give the Tin Man a heart, so he gives him a testimonial. He gives each of them, in a sense, fake evidence that they possess the one thing they want but don't possess at all.

Is this coming into focus now? Can you see why Hollywood might have been attracted to this story of a man who goes to a gorgeous place and becomes the biggest thing in town by conning everybody? Clearly, this aspect of the wizard was so appealing to the filmmakers that they accentuated it in the ending of the *Wizard of Oz* film. In the book, he merely talks the hapless trio into accepting less than they want, but in the movie he gives them actual *lessons* in fraudulence. The three men come to him wanting items of deep, internal, personal value, and he more or less tells them forget it, you don't need it, just take the stuff I give you and go off and fool people. In this world, you don't need to present yourself truthfully. You just need a good front.

THE WIZARD OF OZ **IS A GREAT FILM.** This much has been recognized since at least the 1950s. It debuted to good reviews in 1939 and was considered important enough to be nominated for an Academy Award. But it was not until it started being screened annually on television—back in the days when all TVs were black-and-white—that *The Wizard of Oz* established itself as a classic.

It has an absolutely enchanted first hour, a serviceable third act, and one of the great sequences in movie history (the one that begins with Dorothy's crash landing into Oz and ends with her departure on the yellow brick road). And it features what must rank as one of the best lyrics of all time:

> You're off to see the Wizard
>
> The wonderful Wizard of Oz.
>
> You'll find he is a whiz of a wiz
>
> If ever a wiz there was.
>
> If ever, oh ever, a wiz there was
>
> The Wizard of Oz is one because
>
> Because because because because because
>
> Because of the wonderful things he does.
>
> You're off to see the Wizard,
>
> The wonderful Wizard of Oz.

That's a beautiful, festive, flowing, and intricate little rhyme, even if its contents make us wonder, later, why the Munchkins are so bullish on the wizard's omnipotence. Does he have a publicist feeding fake items to the Munchkinland press?

Yet for all the attention the film has received in the decades since its release, and all the writing that has been done on the subject, not enough has been said about the movie's relationship with its birthplace—which is to say not Kansas, where the story begins, nor upstate New York, where Frank Baum was from, but Hollywood. This is odd because, in a way that seems incredibly obvious, the 1939 *Wizard of Oz* is a movie so much *of* Hollywood that it's practically *about* Hollywood. Whether conscious, unconscious, or semiconscious in its origins, the finished product is yet another Hollywood film about itself.

Seen today, what's generally astounding about the movie is that the means of it are both intricate and visible. The level of craft is considerable but clearly unreal—artisanal-looking. This works to give the movie a timeless, postmodern feel, as though one were looking at handmade puppetry.

Dorothy lands in Munchkinland, where you can see the five o'clock shadows on the Munchkins. They all look vaguely sinister, and the strangeness—more than a fairy tale strangeness, but rather the strangeness of the truly uncanny—is compounded by the beautiful, toy-like sets. Judy Garland, who played Dorothy, was a sixteen-year-old playing a girl who, according to the book, is no more than twelve. So we have a teenager masquerading as a young child, which is weird—a weirdness made achingly poignant by Garland's soul of disturbing vulnerability. The fact that we now know that MGM was binding her breasts and stuffing her with amphetamines projects an extra shadow onto the on-screen event.

So this is Hollywood's version of the Garden of Eden, a place where the Tin Man's eyes are notably bloodshot. Dorothy meets Ray Bolger as the Scarecrow, Jack Haley as the Tin Man, and Bert Lahr as the Cowardly Lion, and you can sense the tired vaudevillians underneath the surface of the extreme costumes. They all do really good work—timeless work, work that has guaranteed them their own slice of screen immortality. But what gives it all a campy creepiness is the sense of strain that comes across. One gets the same impression from Billie Burke as Glinda, who is a good twenty years too old for the part and plays the role as though she were, in some hard-to-define way, mentally defective. The old pros are all in there swinging nonetheless, muscling their way to another honest day's work on the entertainment chain gang.

Like sweat making rivulets down the face of a clown, the interface between tawdry and pretend is all too visible, and yet the imaginative effort is total. Past the age of innocence, you are never *not* aware of the factory that made the movie, even if you can occasionally push that awareness to the edge of your mind. As with a circus, you watch both the performance and the strenuousness of the investment.

The movie, which seems to resonate on a level of real time and real place, feels like it's talking more about itself than about Baum's book. The Tin Man wants a heart, but he pronounces it "hot," as though he were from Boston. The Cowardly Lion is clearly not from the forest but from New York City. And the Scarecrow sounds like he's from a part of the country where they might actually have scarecrows. The actors all bring their real voices to the proceedings, which further makes you aware of this gathering from distant places to the dream machine, which is the film itself. What an epic effort it was to make it, almost as if Munchkins died during the filming. They didn't, but Buddy Ebsen, the original Tin Man, almost did. The aluminum dust in the Tin Man makeup put him in the hospital, and he had to be replaced. Even not knowing that, one can feel something grim and ritualistic about the movie, that it's by and about a place where dreams turn into nightmares.

IN BAUM'S BOOK, DOROTHY REALLY GOES TO OZ. In the movie, she just dreams that she did. In Dorothy's dream, the people she knows in real life are turned into things they are not, with some grotesque and disturbing distortions—such as the dismemberment and reassembly of the Scarecrow and the partial burning of the Scarecrow. He is the character Dorothy loves best, and he's the one the audience invests in the most. He's the first friend she makes on the road to Oz, and the face that is most available and accessible to us through the costume.

So just to summarize: The movie tells a story in which Dorothy leaves home, but then turns back. During a tornado, something hits her on the head, and she proceeds to have an elaborate dream that scares the hell out of her. Afterwards she resolves never to leave home again. That about covers it, except . . . why does she leave home in the first place? It's important to remember this—the one thing that, by the end, entire audiences invariably forget.

If you recall, Dorothy starts the movie in a frenzy. Miss Gulch, the richest and most evil human being she knows, has resolved to kill Dorothy's dog. It gets even worse: As we soon find out, the authorities—perhaps reluctant to offend the town's richest citizen—have issued an order for Toto to be seized and, as Miss Gulch puts it, "destroaaayed!"

What does Dorothy's family do about it? Well, they're useless. Auntie Em and Uncle Henry are both close to a hundred years old, and both are terrified of authority. What's worse, the Uncle is terrified of Auntie Em. How Dorothy ended up not with parents or even grandparents, or even people that look like siblings of her parents, but with what seem to be relatives of her *grandparents*, is never explained, but it implies a serious and disturbing death rate in Dorothy's family. In any case, Uncle Henry is a genial waste of space, and Auntie Em is just plain nasty. With one exception at the end, Auntie Em never lets Dorothy finish a sentence. She is constantly cutting her off. And when the crisis comes—when Miss Gulch and her minions in the local government decide to kill Dorothy's dog—Auntie Em and Uncle Henry do nothing.

So, of course, Dorothy runs away—and we get the tornado, the head injury, etc.—until finally, after a long (fantasy) adventure, she wakes up in her own bed. Dorothy tries to tell everyone her dream, but, as you may have noticed when you've tried to tell people *your* dreams, no one wants to hear them, ever. (Here's a pro tip: When people's nostrils flare as you talk to them, it means they're suppressing a yawn.) Finally, the movie ends with Dorothy's announcement that she is never leaving Kansas, and that there's no place like home, and everyone who has ever watched the movie gets a warm feeling inside.

Except, it must be pointed out . . . *nothing has changed since yesterday.* The witch is dead, but Miss Gulch is alive, and no bucket of water will get rid of her. Five minutes after the movie ends, they probably come and kill Dorothy's dog.

But hold on, you might think: Isn't Dorothy more equipped for dealing with Miss Gulch as a result of her imagined adventure? There's an obvious answer to that: *No.* She has no ruby slippers. She has no power at all.

But what about Auntie Em? Won't she fight harder for Toto now that Dorothy has shown a willingness to leave home over the issue? Again, *no.* Nothing in Auntie Em's behavior indicates any deepening of awareness, and even if she were motivated by pure self-interest—a desire to see Dorothy not run away again—that concern is now off the table. Dorothy has already said she is not leaving, and she looks like she means it.

Of course, we can interpret the ending of *The Wizard of Oz* in a more fanciful way. One might say, for example, that Kansas is no more home than Oz is. Home is knowing that you are enough. Home is knowing that the quest that takes you into the realms of fire and ice is internal, and that being enough in oneself is the overarching message. The dog and Dorothy's affection for him can even be seen as emblems of the unadulterated true self.

Yet none of that eliminates Dorothy's problem as spelled out in the first scenes. And whether or not you believe that the movie ends with Toto just days or hours away from a pair of unwanted injections, this much is certain: In Kansas, someone is determined to kill Dorothy's dog, while in Oz the one person who wanted to kill Toto has gone where the goblins go, below, below, below . . .

Why dwell on this? Quite simply, because the truth of the film—the truth of its message—is contained in this thunderously important yet often ignored and unnoticed plot detail. Here is a Hollywood movie from 1939 that insists on telling us all, children and adults alike, that home is so wonderful that we should never leave it—ever. Yet it presents home as the place where *they want to kill your dog*, and it forgets to resolve that plot detail.

Resolving it would have been easy. Professor Marvel, when he sticks his head in and checks on Dorothy, could have mentioned that a house fell on Miss Gulch. That would have taken care of her. But the filmmakers chose not to do that, because the whole *real* point of the movie is that Dorothy has it exactly wrong: Home is horrible. Oz is horrible, too, populated by evil witches, oblivious good witches, useless charlatans, menacing munchkins, and evil flying monkeys. But at least it's in *color*. At least it's exciting. At least the law won't side against a dog. At least you don't have a team of ancient relatives lurking about to make you feel guilty for wanting to breathe.

All these years later, it's impossible to know for sure if this was the intentional message of *The Wizard of Oz* or if it's simply a product of a film culture that believed so little in home and so much in Hollywood (and in the life of the imagination) that it just couldn't fake it. If I were to guess, I'd say the latter. It was, after all, a production of MGM in the late 1930s, where sanctimony had become something of an artistic reflex, something automatically used to paint over real and unconscious impulses. "There's no place like home" was just the usual propaganda.

In any case, whether intentional or unintentional, the true and obvious message of *The Wizard of Oz* has been hiding there in plain sight for more than eight decades: Hollywood is merciless, awful, and dangerous, but it's way better than home.

I WOULD ARGUE THAT THIS DISHARMONY between the movie's real message and its ostensible message is a big part of what makes *The Wizard of Oz* a great film. It forms a kind of nagging undertone, a hint of complication, a strange "other" feeling amidst the general mirth. True, almost no one who sees the movie comes away consciously fretting over Toto's odds of making it through the week. That's just me. But *every* person who sees it feels a vague sense of loss, which might translate into a conscious feeling of missing Oz, for example, of wishing the magic could be real. In my own experience, I know that, as a child, I misremembered the ending, and I can still see, vividly, a scene that I apparently created in my own imagination: Everyone clears out of Dorothy's room and she gets out of bed and . . . lo and behold, she's wearing the ruby slippers!

But my ending would not have been as good as the one the filmmakers created. My ending is happy and nothing more. It simply affirms the magic and promises a sequel. The real ending creates a mix of feelings—of happiness, sadness, loss, joy—the sense of something irretrievable, of a lost paradise that Dorothy was albeit lucky to escape and yet will miss for the rest of her life.

This is often how we feel at the end of a truly great movie, exhilarated and yet wistful, a bit forcibly kicked out of Eden, like we got close to another world and now have to go home. It's a feeling of not quite knowing what happened to us, as if the world has gotten bigger but we can't quite see how. Like great wine, great movies have a complex finish. Not an *ambiguous* finish—ambiguity is saying nothing, vaguely—but a complex finish that communicates lots of things at once.

I liken this to the way a chord works in music. Most movies end on a single note, but great movies—like *The Wizard of Oz* and *La La Land* and *Queen Christina* and *Casablanca* and *No Country for Old Men* and Zeffirelli's *Romeo and Juliet* and *Blue Is the Warmest Color* and *Mr. Smith Goes to Washington* and *Once Upon a Time . . . in Hollywood*—end on a chord. One tone dominates, but there are other tones that resonate in our ears and emanate in other directions.

And all this is related to that thing we call genre. After all, what is genre, anyway? It's simply a concession to the smallness of art and the hugeness of life. We admit going in that life on Earth cannot be encapsulated by a single work of narrative art. Sometimes artists try—Tolstoy, with *War and Peace*, gave it his best shot— but life is too big to be contained. Thus, there's genre. The novelist, playwright, or filmmaker walks up to the reader or the audience and more or less says, "Okay, let's make a deal. We all know I can't express the whole of life here. So, for convenience, let's just agree that life is funny. And in return I'll give you a world in which life is funny, and in which nothing will seriously intrude on that viewpoint. Or we can decide that life is serious, or life is adventurous, or suspenseful, or thrilling . . ."

Genre is at heart a necessary means by which we lower our expectations, agree to a limit in the range of what will be depicted, and in return we get a world that makes sense and a story that, we hope, says something valuable from within that constraint.

Well, great films, in a sense, *transcend* genre. They end as they must end, without violating the genre promise, but their endings suggest more. They make us feel the bigness of life. They can't contain or fully express the bigness of life, because nothing can, but a great work throws a shadow larger than itself, and we feel expanded in ways we don't expect and can't explain.

Now a great artist, like Charlie Chaplin, can make such an ending happen by intent—for example his ending for *City Lights* (1931). But I believe that, in movies, the complex finish most often happens through lucky accident. And so, in the late 1930s, there were people living in Southern California, within the bubble of the movie industry, stuck inside that Hollywood ethos, trying to tell a sweet children's story, and they ended up transcending the fairy tale genre.

They didn't mean to, but California sneaked in between the frames, and *The Wizard of Oz* ended up lovely, but a little bit sick—and a masterpiece.

IN MODERN MOVIES, this notion that Hollywood is awful but better than real life has been best expressed by director Sofia Coppola in a number of films. As the daughter of a massively important and powerful director and producer, Coppola knows this world, including everything bad about it. Yet even knowing all the awfulness, her own personal response has been not to go wandering into the desert, or to join a convent, but to become a movie director herself. And this life choice has parallels in the films she's made.

Lost in Translation (2003) is about a young woman (Scarlett

Johansson) who befriends a famous (if somewhat declining) movie star (Bill Murray) in Tokyo, where he has gone to make $2 million filming a whiskey commercial for the Japanese market. The movie star is depressed and melancholy, but the movie has the honesty to not pretend that he'd be any better off were he *not* a movie star. He remains, for us and the young woman, a figure of mystery and glamour, someone in possession of important wisdom about life.

Sofia Coppola's usual pattern is to show us people who are lucky beyond our wildest dreams of ego and avarice, and then she tells us that they're miserable. Not only that, but she proves it with convincing examples so we can believe that, were we to switch places with them, we would be miserable, too—maybe not that *day*, but after a long-enough interval, during which we'd get used to and bored by the privilege.

In Coppola's *Somewhere* (2010), a morose and discontented film actor (Stephen Dorff), a megastar on the scale of Brad Pitt in his thirties, takes up residence in a hotel, where he hires twins to do pole dances in his room. He tests a sports car. He mopes, and wherever he goes, women smile at him. He doesn't have the dignity of having it bad, and he doesn't have the pleasure of having it good. At one point, he laments that he's "not even a person." But would he trade places with anyone normal? No, because then he'd have it worse.

The insight here seems to be that having everything means feeling less, and that having such a big life—full of every earthly temptation and all the possibilities of limitless stimulation and a constant flow of new people—can put one outside the realm of normal comforts, such as family. It creates the illusion of revelation that nothing and no one is really important because everyone and everything is replaceable. Yet here again, Coppola's honesty as an artist leaves open an even darker possibility, that this is no false revelation at all. Rather, this vision of utter futility and meaninglessness could be the revealed truth and just another example of the ways in which a privileged existence provides insight—a first-class seat with an unobstructed view into a very real abyss.

If looked at that way, no one in possession of the fruit of knowledge would give it up in favor of ignorance. Okay, maybe *someone* might, but absolutely no one would give up the fruit of knowledge for the blue plate special of ignorance, obscurity, and poverty. Even under the worst of circumstances, it's still better to be a movie star. All good Hollywood movies end up telling you that, one way or the other, because no one who has ever made a movie with a budget over five cents has ever really believed otherwise.

Judd Apatow's *Funny People* (2009) touches on, as if only in passing, some of the same issues. It's the story of a successful comedian and film star (Adam Sandler) suffering from a potentially fatal disease, but along the way, shows how a person of such stature lives his life. For the most part, he has a dream existence of first-class travel and limousines, and everywhere he goes he's met by simpering, groveling inferiors. But he has lost all the friends he had before he was famous, and no one he has met since can react to him as a normal human being. Even worse, all this privilege is to some degree corrupting, because the truth is that he really doesn't want to be treated like just another person. He may resent being treated as something apart but, given the choice, he would never give up his exalted status. Again, the Hollywood life isn't good, just better than everything else.

HOLLYWOOD IN HOLLYWOOD MOVIES is the land of Oz—cruel, dangerous, but wonderful, offering delights and satisfactions that are entirely unique. The movies either start with this assumption or arrive at it, even if the paths they take or their shadings of message are entirely different. *The Artist*, the wonderful silent movie released in 2011, depicts a silent film star's fall from grace and subsequent return. The fall is deeply painful, and the return is ecstatic, like readmittance into paradise. We can relate this to Gene Kelly's dance to the title number in *Singin' in the Rain* (1952). It is remembered as a brilliant set piece, but within the film it's presented as an expression of blissful relief—it comes at the point that a silent star realizes that he will be able to continue in his career. Meanwhile, in Preston Sturges's *Sullivan's Travels* (1941), a comedy director, after a long crisis of purpose, followed by imprisonment on a false charge, resumes his old career, with a renewed commitment to making people laugh. He decides that it's a good life, helping people by making movies.

We can go on and on like this, with examples that affirm Hollywood's ultimate value, worthiness, or desirability. But special note must be taken of Quentin Tarantino's fantasy reimagining of the Manson murders in *Once Upon a Time . . . in Hollywood* (2019). It ends with a veteran Western star killing members of the Manson family; whereupon he is invited to the house of his neighbor, Sharon Tate—an invitation we're led to believe will probably boost his career. It's an ending that, like the ending of *The Wizard of Oz*, has the type of complexity we associate with great films. Though we feel good that the characters have arrived at a happy ending, we might also notice that, by the movie's last moments, our exhilaration at witnessing the slaughter of the Mansons has already faded. Now reflective and not merely reactive, we are back to remembering what *really* happened that night in 1969, and that Rick Dalton (Leonardo DiCaprio) and his stunt man (Brad Pitt) are fictional characters, and that Sharon Tate and her friends experienced horrific and unspeakable deaths.

We wish life could be like the movies, but we know that it's not. We wish Hollywood could be like Hollywood in the movies. We clutch at the fairy tale, the "once upon a time," but we don't believe it, but we want to believe it, and we're comforted by it, even as we don't believe it.

We are sad and happy at the same time, clicking our heels together and saying, "There's no place like Hollywood, there's no place like Hollywood . . ."—and then opening our eyes to see that we haven't gone anywhere.

CHAPTER TWO
The Glory of Youth

In real life, great nights can happen anywhere. But in the movies, they happen in California.

Now, for the record, there have been "one-great-night" films set outside California. Richard Linklater pretty much started his career with one (*Dazed and Confused* [1993], set in Austin), and eventually made two of the best ever filmed, *Before Sunrise* (1995), set in Vienna, and *Before Sunset* (2004), set in Paris. And in 2008, there was the Peter Sollett film *Nick and Norah's Infinite Playlist*, set in New York City.

But most one-great-night films are set in California, perhaps partly out of convenience—the movie industry is based there, after all—and partly because these movies usually need to cover lots of ground in a short time, so a place with a car culture is essential. But most significantly, California is famously the land of taking a chance and getting rich quick, and these movies are an analogue to that.

Sometimes the equivalent of striking it rich is falling in love. Sometimes it's discovering one's own strength and identity.

Sometimes striking it rich actually does have something to do with money, and sometimes it's a combination of all these elements. But whatever an individual movie's definition of success might be, the California one-great-night movies are all about individual transformation, about taking a chance and reaching some wonderful, assured place within oneself.

This idea of becoming the best version of yourself that you can be is the extra ingredient that California brings to these stories. It's the essential difference between California movies such as *American Graffiti*, *Modern Girls*, and *Superbad* and non-California efforts such as Linklater's *Before Sunrise* and *Before Sunset*.

The distinction is worth making because it's instructive. The first two of the three *Before* movies, for example, are all about falling in love. They're not about self-realization *through* love. They're not about people finding out who they are as a result of taking a chance. The protagonists of the *Before* films, Celine (Julie Delpy) and Jesse (Ethan Hawke), are already realized and entire in themselves. They meet as complete people and discover (or, in the case of the second movie, *rediscover*) that they are soulmates.

The California movies are more about discovering a love of life through an encounter with the unexpected, with danger, with fun, with taking a chance—all of which can *include* love, but love's not the end of it. In a sense, these films are about people who find that they now *can* love because they've overcome fear and doubt and have become better people. They have made the emotional equivalent of riding their horse from the East Coast to California, and now they're tougher, better, and happier.

The opening music to *Swingers*, the 1996 Doug Liman film

that introduced Jon Favreau and Vince Vaughn, is the Dean Martin song "You're Nobody 'Til Somebody Loves You." The point of these California movies is a variation on that: "Nobody's gonna love you until you become somebody, and becoming somebody is becoming a whole person, and becoming a whole person is an inner process."

Yes, exactly. Very California.

IN JANUARY OF 1977, the Runaways—an all-girl band from Los Angeles—released their second album, *Queens of Noise.* The Runaways were around my age, either seventeen or eighteen, and I'd liked their first album a lot. So, when my classes were over the day the album came out, I walked a few blocks from my high school to Your Music Center, which was absolutely the best record store in Staten Island. There was a sign in the window— the owner had gone to lunch and would be back in an hour—and so I waited.

Few things are as forgettable as weather, except when it's really, really nasty, and this day was absolutely freezing. I was wearing a hat, gloves, a parka, a sweater underneath, but nothing could keep the cold out. It was too cold to sit still, so I walked around, but not too far, because I didn't know when the guy would be back. (I didn't know when his "hour" began and when it would end.) Plus, I knew that for a comparative novelty item like the Runaways' second album—in terms of popularity, they weren't exactly Zeppelin—he'd probably have only one or two in stock, and I didn't want to walk away for twenty minutes only to have someone else grab my copy.

So I paced back and forth outside, not for an hour but for almost an hour and a half, until, finally, the guy showed up, jangling his keys. I bought the album, took the bus home, went up to my room, and put it on. And as I slowly thawed out, I heard lead singer Cherie Currie singing "California Paradise," about "all night parties" and "loud guitars" and how "California summer never ends." And I thought, "Am I a moron? Why am I here? Why am I not at that party with Cherie Currie and Joan Jett?" By the tenth time I heard the song, I was thinking, "I have to go to California."

Eventually, spring came, and with spring, the thought faded. I did end up going to California, but by other means, and I didn't go to Los Angeles—or "wicked Hollywood," as they say in the song—though that's exactly where I would have headed when I was seventeen. In any case, in that moment—half frozen, in the depths of a bleak New York winter—I got the message that movies and the culture had been dishing out all my life, except this time I felt it. This time I believed: *It's good to be young, but it's great to be young in California.*

Which brings us to a moment in *Less Than Zero,* when Robert Downey, Jr., drops off his friend, Andrew McCarthy, at LAX airport. McCarthy is about to start college in the Northeast. As McCarthy gets on the moving walkway that will take him to his fate, Downey calls after him, sarcastically telling him that he's heading for a great time of "hot cocoa, girls with woolen knee socks, . . . long, leafy walks, girls with flannel nightgowns, L.L. Bean." Three months (but a few minutes of screen time) later, McCarthy returns to Los Angeles for the holidays, and on the drive from the airport he looks up at the palm trees lining the streets, and the audience needs no explanation. This is California, and not only is this better than long, leafy walks, but this place is balmy and beautiful even at Thanksgiving.

As anyone who has ever seen *Less Than Zero* knows, it hardly presents a positive vision of life among the young and well-off in L.A. It's a portrait of addiction, of spiritual desolation and emptiness. I used to think that it's a weakness of the film that it makes decadence and misery attractive all the same, but that's really the whole point—and illustrative of the paradox that's part of the Los Angeles seduction, where you end up seeing the beauty in emptiness and wanting to live inside an illusion.

In that same movie, there's a moment when Andrew McCarthy and Jami Gertz are kissing in a convertible, stopped in the middle of a busy suburban street, and a bunch of guys from a motorcycle club whiz by on both sides of the car. Suddenly, they're all part of the same moment in a seemingly wonderful and crazy city. Like so many moments in California movies, it crystallizes a perfect, fleeting, and glorious moment of youth.

Stories about the gloriousness (and sometimes the pain) of youth often play out over a compressed period of time. *Romeo and Juliet* takes place over six days, and, as I've mentioned, many movies get it done in one. These compressed narratives emphasize the ephemeral nature of youth, as if it lasts no longer than a moment, and they accentuate the preciousness of these transformative moments.

One of the best examples of this kind of film, California style, is *Modern Girls*, which deserves to be better known. Directed by Jerry Kramer and written by Laurie Craig and Anita Rosenberg, this 1980s time capsule opened in theaters in December of 1986 without first having been screened for critics. As a result, it came and went with almost no publicity, and for years it wasn't available on DVD or Blu-ray. It is, to be sure, lightweight and occasionally obvious, but all the same it has the magic that these films sometimes achieve. It captures its cultural moment and, in a mere eighty-four minutes, somehow shows each of its four main characters transforming and deepening as a result of this one great night.

Along the way, it becomes a tour of the Los Angeles club scene, but not in the way you'd expect. It's not a tour of specific clubs but an encapsulation of an era's dream of the nightclub. Everybody's cool. Everybody's there. Everything is possible.

It begins when average-guy Cliff (Clayton Rohner) shows up at an apartment for a date with the very beautiful Kelly (Virginia Madsen) only to find she has stood him up to be with her ex-boyfriend, a smug deejay. Because she took the car, her roommates, Cece (Cynthia Gibb) and Margo (Daphne Zuniga), need Cliff, since he can take them to a nightclub. From that thin premise begins the sequence of personality clashes, inconveniences, and near disasters that somehow add up to the best night of their lives.

Early in the night, Cece meets the British rock idol Bruno X, and he falls immediately in love with her, but then they're separated—in an era before cell phones!—when police raid the bar. Interestingly, Bruno is played by the same actor who plays Cliff, but I've shown this movie to lots of people, and it's rare that anyone watching it notices this detail until the last two minutes of the movie. The first time I saw it, I didn't either.

Anyway, for a long stretch of *Modern Girls*, the characters are in search of Bruno X, and for another part of the movie they're trying to rescue Kelly from a creep who might assault her. Over the course of all this forward motion, the various characters draw closer. Cece, at the last minute, decides not to go off with Bruno on his private plane; Kelly realizes she needs to stop involving herself with bad men; and Margo and Cliff embark on a relationship. The last line of the film sums it up: Cliff turns to the women and says, "What are we doing tonight?" and they start laughing and slapping him. It's hard to imagine anything more happening than has already happened.

Modern Girls is in the category of film that usually can't be appreciated in its own era because it so embodies the era that few people living in that time can recognize its specialness. Add in the fact that it's rough and ungainly, that its seams show, and that it was probably never intended to be anything other than a clothesline for a soundtrack, and you can see why the film has never gotten much of a hearing. But I see a roughhewn classic worthy of discovery, as well as one of the ultimate California one-great-night films. It also neatly fulfills the promise of the subgenre, in that it's about finding love and, even more, about finding oneself in the process.

By the end of *Modern Girls*, it's hard to know whether everything worked out for the characters *because* of Los Angeles or in spite of Los Angeles. This is often the case with L.A.-based romances: In some way, it's understood that people find their partners and themselves by subverting or ignoring L.A.—its madness, its coldness, its dangers, its impersonality. Yet even in those cases, you (and presumably they) have to wonder: If the city weren't so crazy, would they have had the adventures that brought them together?

Precisely such a love-hate relationship with Los Angeles is a major presence in *Swingers*, which begins with a montage of all-night diners and hard-looking waitresses, the suggestion of a lonely world. In that world, we meet Mike (Jon Favreau), who left the East Coast to become a stand-up comic. His career has stalled, and he pines for his old girlfriend, who is still in New York. Meanwhile, his friend Trent (Vince Vaughn) keeps encouraging him to go out and meet women, and much of the comedy comes out of the various ways Mike manages to sabotage himself with every woman he encounters.

There's a lot to say for this film—the set piece, in which he calls a woman's answering machine over and over, has become a classic—but for our purposes, the point of interest is the relationship between the central character and Los Angeles. He goes out every night looking for women and at one point complains, "I spent half the night talking to a girl who was looking around the room to see if there was someone in the room more important to talk to."

In one scene, he approaches a woman at a party, and before he can say anything, she asks what kind of car he drives. "A Cavalier," he says, and she turns away and ignores him. So, having learned that lesson, he next presents himself to a woman as more successful than he actually is. But she recognizes him as someone who applied to work at Starbucks the week before.

Eventually, nonstop failure has the effect of beating Mike into authenticity. He stops playing the Los Angeles game and leads with his true self and ends up meeting somebody in a way that feels natural and easy. At one point the new woman in his life asks, in passing, where he parked his car, and he gestures, "It's that red piece of shit over there." The idea seems to be that he has become his authentic self *within* Los Angeles, and he's stronger for the experience *because* of Los Angeles. Maybe he has found lasting love and maybe he hasn't. That doesn't matter. The victory of the movie is the central character's victory over himself. This makes *Swingers* a very California movie, as well a one-great-night movie with a difference. It gives us the one great night, but only after a succession of bad ones.

The 1999 film *Go* is a departure from most one-great-night films, but the vision of Los Angeles has similarities to *Swingers*, perhaps because the films have the same director, Doug Liman. Sarah Polley played Ronna, a cashier who is short on the rent and so spontaneously decides to make herself the go-between in a drug deal in order to raise the money. This leads to an insane cascade of complications, car crashes, injuries, and a couple of shootings, ending with Ronna limping back to work, with money to pay the rent.

In this film, the debut of screenwriter John August, we get a Los Angeles that's aggressive and harsh, in which anything can happen, where people are selfish and pursuing their interests in a thoroughly amoral way. To survive, the characters must think on their feet, be resilient, and meet the city on its own terms. Thus, like *Swingers* and a lot of other movies set in Los Angeles, it becomes a kind of tribute in disguise, if only because the people making the movie know—just by virtue of getting to make a movie—that they, like the characters, have survived, too.

This mixed feeling about a place is not a California thing

but a specifically Los Angeles thing. Other cities and towns in the state don't feel like they are in an active conspiracy to kill you and don't position themselves in implicit opposition to normal human aspiration. Take, for example, *Gameel Gamal*, a 1976 short film by Gordon Inkeles that played a number of film festivals before disappearing, until home video revived it more than three decades later. It's about the belly-dance culture that sprang up around San Francisco in the mid-1970s, and it's one of those movies that enshrines youthful moments in golden memory. On some distant but vibrant afternoon, DeAnn Adams (Miss Sonoma County, 1968) performs an extended dance for a lunchtime crowd at the Embarcadero, and you can feel the optimism and exuberance of this moment. What's notable is that the positive mood doesn't clash with the setting. It seems, if anything, an expression of it.

With Los Angeles, this kind of optimism becomes more possible when we get away from the city proper. *La Bamba* (1987), one of a string of strong films that were made about Latinx culture in the late eighties and early nineties, tells the true story of rocker Ritchie Valens's mayfly career. Growing up in a poor family in Pacoima, in the San Fernando Valley, he is discovered, promoted, and becomes a glorious success—and then, at seventeen, is killed in the same 1959 plane crash that also robbed the world of Buddy Holly and the Big Bopper. But before he leaves the Earth, he experiences the California dream—money, self-affirmation, a girlfriend that adores him, a new house for his mother, and, of course, a pale blue Thunderbird convertible whose top never has to come down because the weather in Los Angeles is always, always perfect.

As in many films about Latinx California, there is no cynicism about the dream itself. We're invited, instead, to perceive the California dream from the perspective of the outsider. In the case of the American-born Valens, this child of immigrants was actually perceived as someone from another country—in an early scene, a record company owner assumes that Valens doesn't speak English, when, in fact, he doesn't speak Spanish. It's only when he becomes successful that he is seen in all his specialness and individuality, as someone who fully belongs. This indicates a serious inequity, which the film emphatically does not push out of sight. But *La Bamba* is so alive with the youthful happiness of this moment that other considerations recede to the movie's edges.

There's also the optimism that comes of fleeing the city and heading straight to the coastline. In the beach movie *Gidget* (1959), we feel some of the magic of the environment, which seems to enhance and support the world of youth that it portrays. *Beach Blanket Bingo* (1965)—the most famous of the Frankie Avalon–Annette Funicello movies—tries to do the same, but it comes a bit too late in the 1960s, and it's hampered by the stars themselves. Funicello looks like Avalon's mother, and Avalon goes through most of the movie angry and is barely nice to her (possibly the result of displaced anger toward Mom). The movie makes little use of California—some of it looks like it was filmed in a studio— and even the bathing suits are unattractive. Paul Lynde shows up as a publicist taking pictures of his pop star client (Linda Evans) with a Polaroid camera, therefore no negative, therefore you can't make prints, therefore they can't be used for publicity. (This does put him on the technological cutting edge, however.) It looks like the movie cost eight bucks to make, and it's hard to imagine the source of its reputation all these years later.

SUPERBAD (2007), written by Seth Rogen and Evan Goldberg, has become a classic one-great-night high school movie, enough so that it was answered by another, *Booksmart* (2019), about two high school girls on a last big night before graduation.

Superbad is a warm film about departures. Two friends, played by Michael Cera and Jonah Hill, have been inseparable since childhood, but soon they'll be going to different colleges, and they're going to be separated not just by physical distance but by forces within themselves. They talk incessantly about girls—each has a girl that he's particularly interested in—and most of the film involves the guys trying to buy liquor for a party, which is difficult given that they're underage.

The boys are anxious to enter the world of women, but they don't quite know yet that gains in life are usually accompanied by loss. So the end of the movie finds them at the mall, pairing off with their respective prospective girlfriends. It's a transition they want, and should want; and it's a transition and a success that they achieve in true California style, by taking a chance and opening themselves to inner growth. But it's one that will take them away from each other and this safe period of life that they probably didn't quite appreciate until the last moments of the movie, when they dimly but most certainly realize that they are leaving this stage forever.

To emphasize its connection with *Superbad*, *Booksmart* went so far as to cast Jonah Hill's sister, Beanie Feldstein, in one of the lead roles. Kaitlyn Dever played her shy lesbian best friend. In a story similar to *Superbad*, these studious girls are in search of a party, at which they hope to have all the fun they missed out on over their four years of high school. The film has some funny and extreme incidents, including a chance encounter with a serial killer, and it satirizes the attitudes of well-off Southern Californians.

It also captures the quite real sense that teenagers often have, an awareness of the clock, of living inside their own past. It's as if there are two outs in the ninth and they're down by one run in the World Series of their lives. They know that, however things go, they are fated to remember this moment forever. And so they have to make it count.

The only note of sourness in *Booksmart* is the implicit smugness of the young characters, who, because of their wealth, are guaranteed entrance into fancy schools and a smooth ride for life. The Feldstein character's assertion that "the day of the straight white male is over" hardly makes things better. After all, what straight white males is she talking about anyway? The 99.9 percent of them who were born with considerably less privilege than she has, as a wealthy white girl living in Southern California? The characters' certainty of their own social virtue and wisdom, which the movie treats as axiomatic, intrudes on the comedy, though it does accurately reflect an element of present-day California and may, as a result, make the film valuable as an amusing yet mildly discomfiting time capsule in decades to come.

OF COURSE, THE ULTIMATE CALIFORNIA one-great-night movie is *American Graffiti*, which reached legendary status not long after its release in 1973. Set in the year before JFK's assassination, the film follows an assortment characters cruising the streets of Modesto (it was actually filmed in Petaluma) on the last night before the end of summer. And so for the characters and for America, it's a last moment of innocence and, in a way, a last moment of unclouded happiness.

American Graffiti is a film of sequences and, as such, it is a delicate film, one that depends on the cumulative impact of its various parts to achieve the full effect. It's not a film to be watched in fits and starts on home video; it must be watched straight through, ideally in a theater, and when watched in that way, a certain magic takes over.

The magic extends to the film's look, which is heightened and vivid, full of bright colors and neon against the dark night. This vision of Modesto looks alien to our modern eyes because it's the past—but it has always seemed like a faraway past, even when it was only eleven years in the distance. Writer-director George Lucas understood that those intervening years were a vast cultural ocean, and that ocean has only widened in the ensuing decades.

So we look at this world with the increased attention of visitors, just as the natives, within the movie, approach it, with the increased attention of those who know their time here is short. This injects almost every shot with poignancy, or the potential for it: The characters know they're leaving this world, but we know, as well, that this world, whether they stay or go, will be leaving them. Soon there will be assassinations, and

Vietnam, and cultural divides, and the Beatles, and even—as we now know, watching the movie—*the assassination of one of the Beatles*, not to mention the attempted murder of another. The world was about to get seriously complicated, and it's almost as if the characters intuit that, that they are partly infused with our future consciousness and that of their creator.

The first among equals in the cast is Curt (Richard Dreyfuss), who is ambivalent about leaving for the East the next day to start college. Gradually, we understand the difficulty of his decision, the idea of turning one's back on enchantment for cold weather and cold adulthood. But the beauty of the movie is that, as in *Superbad*, we understand the necessity of this passage, that it can't be avoided. To make things harder, and to symbolize all that will be lost, a beautiful woman in a white Thunderbird blows a kiss at Curt and mouths the words "I love you." He spends the rest of the movie looking for her and never finding her, though when he looks out the window from his seat on the airplane, there's the white T-Bird going down the other fork in the road, without him.

It's not unreasonable to imagine that if *American Graffiti* were made in Lincoln, Nebraska, it might have been almost as effective. But when the characters stand near the plane, with the sun shining on the bright morning, the film conveys the California feeling of the world for the taking, of the moment opening itself to the brave.

It also must be emphasized that this notion of personal growth as the ultimate goal—that love, or even disappointment in love, is merely the *means* of growth—is a very California formulation. It's all there in the wonderful last moment of

American Graffiti, when Dreyfuss turns from the window having seen the Thunderbird driving down the road below. He doesn't look frustrated. It's a moment of wistfulness and expansion.

It hurts, but he has already moved on, and he knows it.

CHAPTER THREE
Fame

For more than a century after the founding of the United States, if you wanted to have a career in the arts, you had to make it in New York. New York City is and has been the center of art, publishing, and theater since the beginning of the country, since even colonial days. But the advent of the movie industry gave America a second locus, and one with an entirely different feeling.

The myth surrounding New York has always been about reaching success by achieving a level of such brilliance and ability that you *had* to be recognized. How do you get to Carnegie Hall? Clue: The answer has nothing to do with ordering a milkshake at a drug store and being spotted by a high-powered agent. New York is all about getting good enough to deserve New York's attention, about challenging yourself against the very best and discovering that you match up. "If I can make it there, I'll make it anywhere." Sure, everyone needs a break, so there's always some luck involved, but in the New York vision, luck is all about being prepared to barge right through when the door finally opens a crack.

The California myth is something different. The California dream of artistic success is related to success as defined in the Gold Rush era: You take a chance and go all the way out there, and maybe you'll hit the jackpot. The odds are against it, but you cannot win if you do not play. And since *somebody* is going to get famous, why not you? It's not about being the best; it's not even about being particularly good. It's about showing up and being good *enough*—and being charming.

How did this happen, this idea that anyone could become a movie star? First of all, the notion came into being because, to some extent, it was true. Although from the beginning there were stars who started out on the stage (Charlie Chaplin, John Barrymore) or who even went to acting school (Greta Garbo), a tremendous number of movie stars entered the business through luck, or luck combined with relentless persistence. Norma Talmadge had a mother who pushed her daughter to present herself at a casting office. Joan Crawford was a dancer and a showgirl. Jean Harlow was spotted by Fox executives while sitting in a car. John Gilbert got a job as an extra.

They didn't earn these opportunities because they could act. We know this for certain because *they couldn't act*, not at first. But they got a chance to improve and grow and learn to act because there was something about them that caught someone's eye and inspired someone's belief. They had . . . something special.

Yet here's the thing about something special. A lot of people have it, particularly when they're young. And something special, however special it may be, is usually only a seed that needs to be nurtured. Almost no one, even the most seemingly natural of talents, arrives fully formed. Marilyn Monroe didn't start out looking like Marilyn Monroe. George Clooney wouldn't have had a movie career if Steven Spielberg hadn't told him to stop wagging his head all the time. It takes a certain degree of arrogance to see oneself as a diamond, but how much arrogance would it take for you to think that you're a diamond in the rough who would benefit exponentially from better lighting, clothes, and makeup? That requires no arrogance at all, just a little hope and a reasonably healthy degree of self-belief.

Indeed, that thing—that "something extra"—is at least as much *about* self-belief as it is about good looks or anything else. Thus, the challenge for the aspiring movie star is to keep believing until it becomes true, because once the belief fades, so does the glow.

And yet how do you fake belief if it's already gone? How do you keep hope alive when you're scared to lose it? Some version of this conundrum has probably crossed the mind of every single person who ever tried to make it in Hollywood, and it's a feature of virtually every movie about the struggle to succeed—the necessity to keep believing. "When your dream dies, you die," Jennifer Beals is told in *Flashdance*.

There's another contributor to this partly true fantasy that anyone can become a star, and that's the democratic nature of stardom itself. We don't feel like we know the pianist performing in concert, or even the great stage actor appearing live in front of us, but movie stars are just like we are, or so we are made to think. In the studio days, they embodied archetypes—each one was practically a personification of a fundamental human quality, like honesty or desperation or wisdom or courage. These people get under our skin and became familiar, almost as familiar as friends, in that we know how they behave, and how they smile, and worry, and think. In the case of old movie stars, we might find ourselves feeling that way about people who died before we were even born.

Yet the experience of stardom is still more immediate than even that kind of connection. It's more intimate. When people look at a close-up, they are looking at someone with the same intensity with which they look at themselves in the mirror. Put George Clooney in close-up at, say, the end of *Michael Clayton* (2007), and then thrust a mirror in front of everyone watching, and a whole audience will gasp in momentary shock at their not being George Clooney.

So movie stars are more than *like* us. They practically *are* us. And thus it takes no leap at all to assume that we have every right to movie stardom, too. All that's required is that we have the courage to go to California while we're young and self-deluded enough to believe we're special. If we can do that, we have every chance of *becoming* special, not only for real but forever.

But above all, getting to California is key, because that's the magic place. That's where a person's fate isn't programmed from birth or proscribed by average abilities. Here, in California, all that matters is how much you want it and how much you *deserve* it for wanting it with such purity and intensity.

AT FIRST, MOVIES TRIED TO PRETEND that we weren't all suckers for this Hollywood thing, that we had better values than all that. In *Ella Cinders* (1926), Colleen Moore played a young scrub woman who goes to Hollywood to become a star and then does.

Her boyfriend from back home happens to show up one day as she's *playing* a scrub woman in a movie, and, thinking he's rescuing her from squalor, he scoops her up and puts her on a train heading for home. The film's director chases the train, and when the boyfriend realizes the truth, he calls to him, "Get a new star to do your scrubbing—we're going to get married."

Yes, in 1926, it was still possible to present that as an unambiguous happy ending: A woman gives up a Hollywood career to marry some bossy guy who couldn't tell a scrub woman from, well, Colleen Moore. But things would soon change. In director King Vidor's very funny Hollywood satire *Show People* (1928), Marion Davies is a small-town girl turned movie star whose fame goes to her head. Her career is beginning to decline, but then the old boyfriend (William Haines) reenters the picture, and he not only brings her back to her senses about resuming their relationship but—this is crucial—*he saves her career.* He gives her back her sense of humor and returns her to her true self, the real, unaffected self that audiences liked in the first place. By 1928, a career and happiness were no longer mutually exclusive. A Hollywood career could be part of a happy life.

A few years later, the drama *What Price Hollywood?* (1932) developed some of the latent ideas in these earlier films and made them explicit. It introduced two questions that had pain underlying them: Can you find lasting happiness as a movie star? And can you find lasting happiness if you *want* to become a movie star but fail? The pain implicit in those questions is the very real possibility that the answer to both is no. You can be bitterly unhappy about never achieving fame, but just as unhappy if you are able to achieve a successful career but then are cast out of that paradise. And as everyone knows (and as actors particularly knew in the early days of Hollywood, before we discovered so many ways to stretch a failing career into infinity), all careers ultimately fade.

What Price Hollywood? told what was to become a familiar story, in which a declining talent meets a rising talent, helps that rising talent rise, and then goes into a slow eclipse. But this turned out to be one of the formula's better treatments. Constance Bennett played an aspiring actress who meets a major Hollywood director, played by Lowell Sherman, at the restaurant where she works. He is unpretentious, a big kidder in a jolly old-Hollywood way and lots of fun. He's also a drunk right at the stage that it's *beginning* to impact his career. He spontaneously takes her to a Hollywood opening and then soon after gets her a screen test, which she blows utterly, not only because she's nervous but because she really can't act. That point is significant. *She wants to be a movie star, but she can't act.*

But she also doesn't give up. She begs for a second chance, and after lots of rehearsal, she nails her second audition and secures a contract. The notion implicit in that is also significant: Even if you can't act, you can learn to be a movie star in a matter of hours or, at most, days, because all it comes down to is relaxing and being yourself. In other words, you're *already* wonderful. You just have to trust it. You have to believe.

The rest of *What Price Hollywood?* traces Bennett's ascent into stardom and the director's descent into alcoholism. In between, there's a marriage between Bennett and a polo-playing stuffed shirt—played by Neil Hamilton, eventually to achieve immortality as Commissioner Gordon on TV's *Batman* and no less stuffy as a young man. The marriage breaks up because Hamilton's character doesn't like the demands of Bennett's career, and, because this was a movie made *before* the Production Code enshrined the dictum that husbands are always right, Bennett remains the sympathetic party. Meanwhile, Sherman, having passed through all the downward stages of self-pity, arrives at the point of ultimate desperation. He stares at a photo of himself looking younger and self-possessed, and then looks at the wreck staring back from the mirror. And he becomes so disgusted that he shoots himself.

In terms of the movie, the suicide makes sense. In these two images, Sherman is confronted not just by the wreckage of his appearance but by what that wreckage shows about his condition in general, that he's hopelessly addicted and has no way out. Still, it's curious and appropriate that, in a Hollywood movie, a man should be driven to suicide precisely by the realization that his looks have gone. This is even more curious when we consider that this was a middle-aged man who was no beauty at any age, and whose career never had anything to do with being pretty. He was a director, not a matinee idol. But there it is: He looks like hell. He sees it. So he commits suicide.

We see the same kind of thing, yet more explicitly, in the classic *Dinner at Eight* (1933). John Barrymore is a former silent film star whose career has tanked with the talkies. (It's hard to see why—his voice couldn't be better—but then in 1933 the only actors left to play former silent film stars who tanked in the talkies were the former silent stars who'd made the cut.) Once known for his handsome profile, the former star has now descended into bitterness and alcoholism. When he makes the mistake of drunkenly abusing his agent (Lee Tracy), the agent lets loose on him. He angrily tells the star that he's through and then points him to a mirror so as to insult him. "You sag like an old woman," he says.

So what does the washed-up movie star do once his agent has left him? He closes the windows, turns on the gas, and arranges himself in a fetching pose for whoever finds the body.

The point here couldn't be clearer: Hollywood success is everything. Life is not worth living without it, whether you're a has-been or a novice. *If you're not famous, you might as well kill yourself.*

This is a sentiment in many Hollywood films, and it takes various forms. It is the California idea that fame is to be valued above all else—above achievement and above a great resume, because a resume is past tense. Don't forget, in the early days, movies were regarded as disposable. When a movie finished its run, it was for all intents and purposes gone forever. There was no television, no VHS, no DVD, no cable, no classic movie stations, and barely any archives. Thus, a movie star was indeed a creature of the present tense, a mayfly in expensive clothing. This in turn made for values that were—and to a large extent remain—all about fame in the moment, about existing in the glow of realized selfhood, even in the midst of knowing that it can't last.

To be a movie star, to have everyone look at you and love you and want to be you and envy you and even half believe for a few fleeting moments that they *are* you—that's the ultimate ego fulfillment, the dream of love for one who has been denied love. Yet, always accompanying even the moments of greatest glory is an agonized knowledge that eventually you will look in the mirror and know that it's over. That others will have decided it already: You're done.

The first *A Star Is Born* (1937) followed close to the pattern of *What Price Hollywood?* A young woman (Janet Gaynor) travels to Hollywood with hopes of making a career, even though she has no particular talent, just lots of enthusiasm and a willingness to learn. She meets Norman Maine (Fredric March), an established movie star—but, alas, an alcoholic—and he gets her the screen test that secures her a career. The key difference is that in this version of the tale they're both young, attractive people, and they get married. She rises, he falls, and, yes, he commits suicide. But the circumstances of the suicide are a bit different, and telling.

When Norman decides to end it all, it's not because he looks in the mirror and doesn't like what he sees. He's Fredric March and barely forty—he looks just fine. No, he decides to kill himself when he overhears that his wife is planning to sacrifice her career to take care of him. That's too much to ask. How could he expect her to give up something precious and irreplaceable, like Hollywood stardom, for something eminently replaceable, such as a husband? So he walks out of their beachfront property and makes straight for the Pacific Ocean, toward a California suicide even more appropriate than going off the Golden Gate Bridge. A product of the ultimate California industry, Norman now returns to the ooze from whence he came.

The second *A Star Is Born*, from 1954, had some subtle differences, in that the singer-actress played by Judy Garland is already a fabulous, undeniable talent when Norman—played this time by James Mason—meets her. Instead of an average young woman with a big dream, she's a dazzling artist who isn't dreaming big enough . . . until Norman opens up the world for her. The motive for the suicide is slightly different as well. Like Fredric March, Mason is in despair when he finds out that his wife is about to give up his career for him, but he is also sad to realize that his *own* career is finished—especially since somehow he didn't quite know. But once he does, it's time for him to swim to Hawaii or die trying.

Again, *if you can't be famous, you might as well be dead.* And if you think about it, that's exactly how Norman Maine *should* feel, given his own values. He's a man collapsing under the weight of the value system that tells him he is worthless if he can no longer be a movie star. It's a value system that hardly needs to be described as twisted. Chances are that you, as you read this, are not a movie star. Neither am I. But I like to think we're doing just fine.

And yet . . . so infected have we all become by Hollywood values that we are unwittingly complicit in every footprint Norman makes in the sand. We watch him returning to the sea in 1936 and going back into the water again in 1954. We see him in the 1976 version, too, played by Kris Kristofferson, and in the 2018 version, embodied by Bradley Cooper. And each time we think that it's a damn shame, but we understand and even agree: After all, in each of the films, the women—played by Janet Gaynor and Judy Garland and Barbra Streisand and Lady Gaga—have achieved that precious state of megastardom and the prize of being glorious before the entire world. No one should be expected to give up such a career—or even postpone its advance—to care for a spouse's life-threatening addiction.

In the Hollywood scheme, which is the California scheme,

which is practically, by now, the American point of view, fame is bigger than anything. It's the greatest gift, certainly the rarest, and if you have fame and hate it, at least you have the privilege of knowing you hate it. You have eaten of the Tree of Knowledge, and nobody else can even get in the garden.

In a similar vein, we get, in 1952, Vincente Minnelli's *The Bad and the Beautiful*, in which a group of artists convenes at an agent's office to hear a pitch from a producer, played by Kirk Douglas. The artists all detest the producer with good reason, and in a series of flashbacks we discover those reasons. One of the members of the group (Lana Turner) is an actress that he seduced and abandoned. Another (Walter Pidgeon) is a director from whom the producer stole a movie. The third (Dick Powell) is a writer that the producer completely screwed over: He wrecked the man's marriage and even initiated a chain of events that inadvertently led to the death of the man's wife.

Yet the twist is that in every case, despite the monumental betrayals, the producer ended up either intentionally or indirectly helping each artist's career. Thus, the cynical ending of the movie (and at least this time the filmmakers *knew* they were being cynical) leaves us with the strong suggestion that the director, the actress, and the writer will be working again with the ruthless producer. What's a wife, after all, compared to Hollywood success?

THE HUNGER FOR FAME IS, if anything, worse today than ever. Social media has only propagated Hollywood's supreme value: If you're not famous, you don't exist. If you're not famous, you not only might as well be dead but sort of already are. It used to be that people went through their lives rarely, if ever, taking photos of themselves. In the twenty-first century, however, the most likely subject of your pictures is yourself. And why are you taking them if not to share them, since a star isn't a star without an audience?

Even worse, you take pictures of your food and post them on Instagram. And then, while you're still eating it, you check to see if anyone "liked" your food picture. (Isn't it enough to like your *own* food?) If no one did, you feel slighted.

Of course, this is insane, and even the people who do this know it's insane. Yet it's as if everyone has enlisted to become an Amway salesman, and the product they're selling is themselves. Except they're not really selling themselves but a packaged version of how they want to be perceived. Meanwhile, the self languishes, constantly awaiting judgment or approval, but really both. Even approval is a form of judgment and can turn ugly very quickly.

Ingrid Goes West (2017) explores these issues with its funny, unsettling, and strangely sympathetic portrait of an Internet stalker, played by Aubrey Plaza. Thumbing through a magazine, she seizes on her next obsession/girlcrush/victim, Taylor (Elizabeth Olsen), a young woman in California with three hundred thousand Instagram followers, who has set herself up as an arbiter of style and fashion. With some money from an inheritance, Ingrid moves to Venice Beach and becomes, like Taylor, a blonde. When she meets Taylor—by surreptitiously stealing her dog and then claiming to have found it—she tries to make herself as much like her idol as she can, never venturing an opinion that Taylor wouldn't approve of.

As in a movie about the pursuit of Hollywood stardom, we end up rooting for Ingrid (Plaza) because she wants what she wants with such intensity. In a movie about Hollywood fame, Ingrid would want the world's love and approval, but here she wants Taylor's respect, seeing it as a conduit to some illusion of glory she can promote on social media. *Ingrid Goes West* takes Hollywood values to the limit, with its spectacle of a woman wanting love from someone not worth it, and wanting fame from people she doesn't know and doesn't care about. And, to make it all worse, she doesn't deserve either.

By the finish, when all her schemes implode, Ingrid ends up realizing the aforementioned California truth—that if she's not famous, she might as well be dead—and acts accordingly. She takes an overdose of pills. But before she does, she records a video suicide note, in which she's completely honest about herself for the first time. She posts it online, and when she wakes up in a hospital, she finds out that she's gone viral. Everybody saw her suicide video. Everybody felt that she was speaking for them. Finally, she's a social media success.

The point, however, is not that honesty pays, or that Ingrid finally found that authenticity works. The conclusion is rather that she finally figured out a way to become famous. She hit on the right formula. She is as sick or almost as sick as ever, but she is happy, because she has what she wants.

La La Land (which was announced the winner of the Academy's Best Picture prize of 2016 by mistake) is more retro in style, harking back to the Golden Age musicals of the 1930s and 1940s, and its concerns are classic as well. It avoids the cliché of the veteran and the novice joining forces and instead tells the story of two young, aspiring talents at the same early stage of their careers. They learn from and help each other.

The title, the locations, and the opening number—dozens of people singing and dancing during a gridlocked traffic jam—establish *La La Land* as a very California story. She is an aspiring actress working in a coffee shop. He is a hotel lobby pianist who dreams of establishing a high-end jazz club. They meet and come together, both sensing that the other has traits that they themselves need. Sebastian (Ryan Gosling) is determined, optimistic, and relentless, but too dogmatic and slightly delusional. Mia (Emma Stone) is adaptive and grounded, but with a tendency for despair. Each takes turns steering the other away from career mistakes.

The climax comes when Mia has an opportunity to land a big role in a major film, and Sebastian has to find her and tell her that this once-in-a-lifetime chance is available to her. She aces the audition and gets the role, and then, in a novel plot turn, the couple faces the fact that they must break up. She has to travel for her career. He has to travel for his. These are the years they must dedicate to making it. The relationship has to go.

We are a far cry from 1926 and *Ella Cinders*, but then *La La Land* believes in the talent of its main characters, something that *Ella Cinders* did not. And we believe in the characters' talent, too, because we see it. We especially see Stone's ability in those audition scenes, where the circumstances of the scene become more palpable than the reality surrounding her.

The difference between *La La Land* and most other films that portray the sacrifice of love in exchange for a great career—and the thing that makes this a great movie—is that the people in the film know as much about life as we do watching them. They know the sacrifice is needed. The script doesn't make it easy by killing off one of them, or by presenting some terrible disparity in values that can't be sustained. The characters are faced with a choice of love or career, and because they have the *same* values, they are realistic enough to know themselves and to know the odds: Love will come again in another form, but the chance for a great career is a once-in-several-lifetimes opportunity.

La La Land also has a beautiful realism about success itself, as when the two see each other years down the line, when she is a film star and married and he has opened the nightclub of his dreams. An earlier film might have been sentimental and suggested that success is a poor substitute for the love that was lost. But *La La Land* is saying something else: That every great advance requires sacrifice, and that even though there is nothing like the joy of first love, there is nothing more important than the fulfillment of one's inner self. Because to lose the self would be to lose everything.

Here again is the California idea—if you're not successful, you might as well be dead—but it has been poeticized into, "If you're not successful, you can't be yourself and therefore cannot love." Or perhaps it's this, that if you're not engaged in the active nurturing of that inner flame, the thing that's lovable within you will go, and the thing that loves will turn sour.

In the gentlest way, in a way that's almost sweet, *La La Land* is coldly realistic about who we are, and where we live.

SO FAR WE HAVE BEEN TALKING MOSTLY about movies in which the central character achieves success but finds that the reality is not like the dream: It's complicated. There's fear. There's struggle. There is watching others fail or fade. Hollywood has been very good over the years at dramatizing the dark side of its own dream. This dark side has been, as we've seen, a standard and recurring subject of movies, even to the point that we might say it's part of Hollywood's own romantic self-mythology, a repeated saga that starts at idealism and ends with a beaten-up type of wisdom. *La La Land* and the Lady Gaga *A Star Is Born* are just new and better examples of this tendency.

But there is a whole other aspect to this California myth as expressed in movies, and that's the vision from inside the nightmare. *La La Land*, after all, is about two extremely lucky people who are not just lucky enough to be talented but lucky enough to catch every break as they climb the ladder. Every person has stories and has seen things and knows something about sadness and sacrifice, but it's different—and quite a privilege—to look back from inside the winner's circle.

There is the vision of failure, too, as well as the gross vision of success having curdled into something grotesque, as in Billy Wilder's *Sunset Boulevard* (1950) and Steven Soderbergh's *Behind the Candelabra* (2013). There's also the dead end—often a moral dead end, not just a career dead end—that comes with lack of talent, as in Paul Schrader's *Hardcore* (1979) and Paul Thomas Anderson's *Boogie Nights* (1997). And there's the cruelty of a business that makes its living off the feelings of sensitive people and the casualties that come of that, as in Graeme Clifford's *Frances* (1982).

Sunset Boulevard is basically the justification for all those suicides in early Hollywood movies. The movie shows what can happen when people allow themselves to live past their own years of glamour and fame. Norma Desmond (Gloria Swanson) is able to do it by staying in a state of delusion about her fan base and career prospects. She has a servant—a former silent film director who seems to have been a lot like Erich von Stroheim and who is, by a wild coincidence, played by Erich von Stroheim—who writes her fan letters (unbeknownst to her) so she can believe she isn't completely forgotten. And she has hopes of starring in Cecil B. DeMille's upcoming production of *Salome*, even though she's fifty, looks sixty, and is crazy as a loon. Without this hope, life would not be worth living.

Norma Desmond is both a creature of and a creation of the movies. If she were a New York stage actress who had enjoyed a great career in her youth, she'd still be working in middle age because (1) the parts would be available, (2) she couldn't have achieved any level of great stardom on stage without real ability, and (3) the adulation for a stage star can never be as lethal or addictive to the spirit as movie stardom. Norma is a product of an industry that confers godlike status on people just for being themselves and looking a certain way—and then that same industry takes away that status, with barely a shrug or whisper, leaving the person to wonder what exactly happened. Especially in the 1920s, when Norma Desmond was popular, stars were encouraged to live in a world of unreality, and their eccentricity was rewarded.

Norma Desmond isn't the protagonist of *Sunset Boulevard*. Rather, it's the struggling screenwriter Joe Gillis (William

Holden), who is down on his luck enough to allow himself into Norma's circle and to accept her gifts. He starts off the movie as a corpse in a swimming pool, and the rest of the movie is a flashback that he narrates from the beyond. He is a study in the consequences of failure (or at least lack of success) as much as Norma is a study in the dangers of stardom. It would seem, in Billy Wilder's vision, that you can't win if you win and you can't win if you lose. But, in fact, the movie does show a path to fulfillment—to be like Cecil B. DeMille, who makes a brief appearance in the film, playing himself. The secret is to be genuinely talented. It's the best armor. All others are bound to get hurt.

In Paul Schrader's *Hardcore*, a Midwestern girl (Season Hubley) goes to California, decides to stay, and disappears into the Los Angeles underworld. When her father, a very distraught George C. Scott, goes to look for her, he finds that she is appearing in short hardcore porn films. Had she stayed in the Midwest, she might have married and expressed her discontent through conventional means, such as gradually becoming an alcoholic. But in California the gap between reality and desire becomes all too painful, because the dream seems to be happening all around or it's being offered just out of reach. The fame disease takes hold, and desire takes possession of the soul.

Boogie Nights is more lighthearted, or at least feels that way. The movie tells the story of the porn industry, beginning during that five or ten minutes in the 1970s when some genuinely believed that pornography might become mainstream art. The movie is about a group of people who constitute Hollywood's version of the Land of Misfit Toys. It's about people who are made almost freakish by a veritable hat trick of misperception—

the depths of their delusion, the shallowness of their artistic aspirations, and the nonexistence of their talent. Once again, lack of talent becomes a sympathetic, human, and almost dignifying detail.

The details change. Styles change, levels of depravity change. But the one constant of these films is their tragic take on the consequences of dreaming without talent. In *Boogie Nights* everyone's life spirals and collapses. At first, they're buoyed up in the porn boom, but then video makes porn cheap and ubiquitous. And they feel artistically compromised, which is of course ridiculous and is meant to be ridiculous.

Behind the California idea that life is only worth living if you're famous—that life has value only to the extent that strangers know about you and care—is a purity of need that connects with everyone in our Hollywood-infected world. And the crazy part of it is that the less the talent, the purer the need, and thus the deeper the investment of spirit.

We feel for them. We might even understand them. Everything is on the table, and there's nowhere else to go.

CHAPTER FOUR

A Wonderful Past and a Nightmare Present

San Francisco isn't bad now, but you should have been there thirty years ago. Thirty years ago, it was amazing.

That idea has been in the air since at least the 1880s, when people first started to look back nostalgically at the days of the Gold Rush, and that same feeling has continued until the present time. The San Francisco of the previous generation is always wild, rollicking, and somehow strangely innocent, while the city of the present is invariably staid, corporate, and a little boring, a pale reflection of the glory days.

But at least it's not Los Angeles, because the Los Angeles of the present? Oh, it's horrible, always. If you want to experience the worst of the modern, just watch a new movie set in L.A.

First, let's consider San Francisco, a strange place with a strange population that needs three full decades to figure out if they were having a good time. We see this tendency in movies going all the way back to 1936 and that year's box office champ, MGM's *San Francisco*, the movie that gave the city its theme song. Before the story even begins, right after the opening credits, an onscreen scroll tells about the dignified city of the then-present, and then invites viewers to imagine this same proper city dreaming of its younger self from thirty years earlier, when it was "sensuous, vulgar, and magnificent."

That's how it is with San Francisco. Its vulgar sensuality always seems ultimately benign, at least from the distance of history, while Los Angeles's decadence remains forever young and forever threatening and disturbing. Is this sense grounded in anything tangible, or is it just a matter of luck—that some cities, like some people, are just so good-looking that they can get away with anything?

The movie *San Francisco* opens with a celebration to ring in the New Year, 1906. We're introduced to a party town on a party night, full of people who know how to have a good time. That's a running theme in 1930s films featuring San Francisco—the idea of it as the place to have fun. Perhaps this was an accurate reflection of the city in this era. Or perhaps it had to do with the fact that, in the twenties and thirties, San Francisco was the place where the movie stars would go to let off steam. For example, in 1921, Fatty Arbuckle had a party at the St. Francis Hotel. Alas, not all parties end well.

How freewheeling is this 1906 San Francisco? A nightclub owner named Blackie (Clark Gable) walks into his club, the Paradise, and a woman waves him over to her table. She kisses him, and when the camera pulls back, we see that her husband is snuggling with another woman. So we get the message, that we've come to a place of no rules. Or, as Blackie's childhood friend, Father Tim (Spencer Tracy) describes it, San Francisco is "the wickedest, most corrupt city, most Godless city in America.

Sometimes it frightens me," he adds. "I wonder what the end's going to be."

But *we* don't wonder. We know our seismological history, that on April 18, an earthquake will come and level the place. So there's an implication here that maybe the earthquake, which is on the way, is being brought on by the residents themselves. For some of this we can thank the Production Code, which mandated that all immorality had to be punished. Thus, if a city is going to be presented as immoral, and that immorality is presented as lots of fun, there has to be a comeuppance. Admittedly, an earthquake and fire that lays an entire city to waste might seem an extreme reaction to some extramarital kissing, but hey, we saw those two, and they were asking for it.

The invisible but heavy hand of the Production Code is a dated aspect of *San Francisco*. So is Jeanette MacDonald's singing, which is lilting and on key but has a way of suggesting, sonically, the kind of person who'd wear a ball gown to the beach. We also can't help but notice a strangeness of the film—that it's a musical in which only one person ever sings, and we don't even want her to. Yet to watch the film more than eight decades since its release is to realize that, whatever its faults, it captures the character of San Francisco in ways that continue to ring true today.

San Francisco is portrayed, for example, as a rather preening, self-conscious city. That's still the case. Residents of other cities take where they live for granted, or at least don't think of the place as having some intrinsic meaning. But San Franciscans are under the impression that their city stands for something, and partly, just in the act of believing that, they make it true. There's a subtle boosterism about the place that's very small town, as well as an occasional sense, vague but there, that everyone is acting a part in some larger civic drama; that everyone, like it or not, is participating in this San Francisco thing, which extends deep into history. The city's technology may be forward looking, but the imagination of the city is perpetually looking back.

The movie also hints at the rivalry with Los Angeles, which continues to this day, though, to be precise, it's a rivalry that's entirely one way. (San Franciscans grumble about Los Angeles the way Mets fans grumble about the Yankees. Meanwhile Los Angelenos, like Yankee fans, are too big to notice there's even a rivalry. To them, the other team just seems quaint.) And so, early in *San Francisco*, a drunk is thrown out of the Paradise, and the bouncer asks, "Where are you from?" The drunk says, "Los Angeles." The bouncer says, "I thought so," and punches him in the face.

San Francisco remains, as well, a city of spontaneity and skin-deep sophistication, of lots of swag but no pretense. The movie's washerwoman who grows up to be the grand dame of Nob Hill society (Jessie Ralph) but never bothers to deny her past sounds very San Francisco, even now.

Best of all, the city, past and present, is nicely embodied in the character of Blackie, who is a rogue and a scoundrel and not big on morals or kind words. And yet there's no one in the movie you'd rather have on your side, or to speak well of you. He's fun-loving and honest, and he has a sentimental streak. He is not eccentric, but he has a curious tolerance of eccentricity and a knowing appreciation of people. He's guarded but not closed off. He knows himself, and he's happy enough with himself, but he has the capacity to grow. Most importantly, Blackie, though tough, is not mean. Whatever is bad about him doesn't run deep—and in those ways he's also like his city.

Every city has its rough side, and every city has its share of cruel people. But the essential character of San Francisco is not cruel. The city's homeless crisis, which has gone on in the city for some thirty years, is partly a consequence of the unwillingness of both the population and the government to execute the kind of heartless policies that were put in place by New York City in the 1990s. The city has never had a collective will to be mean.

Residents of San Francisco actually *expect* life to be nice and for the city government to cooperate in making and keeping things nice. This sense of expectation either gives the city a core innocence or reflects it. In either case, the makers of *San Francisco* captured that core innocence, which is perhaps the main reason why the film, despite its vintage, remains essential viewing for anyone wanting to understand the city's soul.

Of course, for a city in love with its past, with its reflection in the rearview mirror, the present can never quite stack up. In the city's collective imagination, San Francisco was once a dangerous but thrilling place, created by a lot of wild but square-dealing good sports who took a chance and rolled with the vagaries of fortune. They had the right spirit to live there, and so they did— like Miriam Hopkins in the 1935 Howard Hawks film, *Barbary Coast*.

She arrives by boat in the 1850s, with plans to marry her fiancé, who has struck gold. But when she gets there, she finds out that he lost all his money at a crooked gambling club and was killed when he complained to the management. You might expect she'd be devastated to hear this, but after registering some surprise, she announces that she didn't love the guy anyway and doesn't care. "I came here to get something, and I'm going to get it," she says. "San Francisco is no place for a bad loser. . . . I'm staying and holding out my hands for gold. Bright, yellow gold."

Early in the film, one of the characters describes the new San Franciscans arriving from the east. "They've all left lives behind them they didn't like. They all dream of being reborn in the new land."

These lines refer, of course, to the people of the Barbary Coast era, but they might as easily have been referring to California as seen through the eyes of the rest of America in 1935. The population of the state had more than tripled over the course of three decades, and for decades yet to come California would continue to attract people from all over the country willing to shake off the lives they didn't like. The remark might easily also be applied to people in the 1930s who'd come west to be in the film business. For those lucky people who left home and staked everything on the longshot prospect of a film career, Hollywood was the new Gold Rush.

As presented in *Barbary Coast*, the new Californians were independent spirits, too restless to stay home, but willing to abide by a code of behavior, even the bad guys. Edward G. Robinson played Louis, the owner of a strictly crooked gambling club. Without doubt, he's the movie's villain—cheating miners out of their gold and sometimes having people killed in order to hang on to his power. Yet even while retaining his villain status, he does two things at the end of the movie that raise his stock in our eyes. He gives up the woman he loves (Miriam Hopkins) and lets her go to the man *she* loves, at least partly out of some vestigial sense of fair play. And minutes later, when his luck runs out and he is about to be hanged by a vigilante group, he faces his fate with equanimity. San Francisco is no place for sore losers.

Perhaps the writers of *The Flame of the Barbary Coast* (1945) were thinking of the earlier movie when, at the end of their film, the villain—another crooked club owner, as well as a city kingmaker, played by Joseph Schildkraut—decides to release his hold on his former lover (Ann Dvorak) and permits San Francisco to have its first free and fair election, even though it means surrendering his stranglehold on power. He's a good loser, too.

WHEN I FIRST ARRIVED IN SAN FRANCISCO in 1985, I often heard from longtime residents that the city was just fine now, but its heyday had passed; the postwar period of the late forties and fifties was when everything had been wonderful. That was Herb Caen's San Francisco, the city that knew how, with a booming economy, beatnik poets, and jazz clubs in North Beach. Now it should be said that in the 1980s, Herb Caen—the dean of San Francisco journalism—was still writing his *San Francisco Chronicle* column and was as popular as ever. And the economy was booming then, too. But no, somehow, the glory days are always gone.

Was this simply the typical nostalgia of middle-aged people? Most of those saying this were older, and some of them may have been remembering their own youths. That's normal and has been the case forever. It's a safe bet that in rural Russia circa 1380, there were fifty-year-old serfs telling the younger serfs that the crops grew faster and princes were kinder back in 1350.

Even so, no one talks with reflexive nostalgia about New York or Los Angeles. No, it seems that this San Francisco nostalgia is something inherent in the place itself. It's either something that the city inspires or else the city itself just happens to consistently attract people who think in this way.

It would be arbitrary to ascribe a reason for this phenomenon, but here's a guess: The city is physically beautiful, but people tend not to see what they look at every day. They're busy, earning a living. But every so often they look up, see the beauty of the place, and yet know they're not really feeling it. They don't have the right sense of flight, of transport. Thus, the nostalgia. It's really just a fantasy that once upon a time they *would* have felt it, and that *everyone* felt it then, that there was once a slightly slower era when the pace of life was in harmony with the physical surroundings.

No? That's not it? Well, again, it's only a theory.

In the 1980s, there weren't many movies looking back on the San Francisco of the generation before, but there was *Heart Beat* (1980), about the friendship of Neal Cassady and Jack Kerouac in the late 1940s and early '50s. Given that it's about the genesis of Kerouac's novel *On the Road*, and those guys weren't exactly stay-at-homes, the movie does move around a lot, but it settles for a long stretch in San Francisco and shows the two men enjoying the nightlife of the era. *Heart Beat* is suffused with the kind of romanticism that can only be acquired through distance. The opening credits are displayed to a rendition of "Love Is a Many-Splendored Thing," presented seemingly without irony.

Actually, you might argue that in the 1980s, San Francisco got a romantic and nostalgic vision of its *own* day, when the crew in *Star Trek IV: The Voyage Home* went back in time to 1986 in search of a whale to bring back to the twenty-third century. All of a sudden, what was then present-day San Francisco looked as magical as San Francisco past, and one can imagine someone seeing that film today, more than three decades later, and gleaning the precise wrong meaning from that—that things really were wonderful in 1986 and that everyone knew it.

In fact, the magic then was exactly as the magic is now, invisible unless you look for it.

IN THE YEARS SINCE, we have seen other films look back on the generation before with wistfulness and reverence. If we want to extend San Francisco's sphere of influence to Silicon Valley, we can detect a nostalgia for the early days of the computer industry in both *Jobs* (2013) and *Steve Jobs* (2015). These films remember a period in which everyone was young, fortunes were to be made, and everything was possible.

But the best recent illustration of the city's nostalgic tendency is *Milk* (2008), about the life of city supervisor Harvey Milk, the gay rights pioneer who was murdered in 1978, along with San Francisco mayor George Moscone. The murders came just nine days after the mass suicide in Jonestown of members of the Peoples Temple, which had been headquartered in San Francisco and where its leader, Jim Jones, had had political support. This double blow rocked the city's sense of itself. A month later, when Philip Kaufman's *Invasion of the Body Snatchers* (1978) was released—it's set in San Francisco—there was a feeling that the film expressed something of the city's reality at the time.

Gus Van Sant's *Milk* doesn't remotely diminish the historic awfulness of the double murder, but it does find *meaning* in it, a sense that social progress came of this tragedy. The movie was released right around the time that public opinion on the issue of gay marriage was beginning to shift, and the movie seemed to suggest the ultimate triumph of the forces that Harvey Milk had set in motion.

The movie evokes the San Francisco of the 1970s as a golden era—a golden era in disguise, perhaps, but still a time of hope and promise. With archival footage that simultaneously brings us closer to that time even as the old film stock reminds us of the era's irretrievability, *Milk* shows the burgeoning days of the gay community in the city's Castro District. There's no need to remind anyone watching that the nightmare of AIDS would, in less than a decade, transform this community. We can't help but be aware of that and therefore look upon the San Francisco of the 1970s, which saw itself as anything but innocent, as an innocent age.

The film ends with a torchlight vigil honoring the lives of Milk and Moscone—an ending that doesn't intentionally but inevitably evokes the end of *San Francisco*, with its vision of a strong people who, in the aftermath of disaster, are going to come together and make things better. These people can be stopped individually, but not collectively. They are right, decent, and noble, and they can't lose.

This is the San Francisco of the movies. A city in love with itself. A people in love with themselves as San Franciscans, but all the same, a benign collective force in the world, always uneasy about the future but taking solace in the lessons of the past. The consistency of these portrayals is either a reflection of an intrinsic reality or evidence that San Franciscans have been imitating San Francisco movies since the 1930s. Considering that this is San Francisco we're talking about, the latter is not entirely impossible.

IT'S HARD TO SAY WHETHER LOS ANGELES or New York is the premier city for depictions of the awful present, but whichever isn't first is second. That Los Angeles is an emblem of the horrible now seems so manifest that examples are hardly necessary. They include at least half of all the film noirs ever made, plus every film about how awful the movie business is. And every crime film set in the hood. And *To Live and Die in L.A.* (1985) . . . Belaboring this with examples would be tiresome.

It might be more instructive, instead, to look at the differences between the New York variety of horrible and Los Angeles horrible. For example, New York horrible is usually practical, while Los Angeles horrible tends to have a philosophical component. New York horrible presents problems that can't be fully solved; Los Angeles horrible often presents a spiritual condition at the heart of what's horrible. Usually, L.A.'s problems can't be solved at all.

Serpico (1973), with Al Pacino, can only make sense in New York and would make no sense at all if set in L.A. In *Serpico*, the city is in the toilet, everything is ugly, and all the cops are on the take—except for this one good guy, who gets shot in the face and yet survives and makes everything in New York ever so slightly better.

Conversely, *Falling Down* (1993), with Michael Douglas, could only have been set in Los Angeles: An average man, stuck in a traffic jam, suddenly snaps, walks away from his car, and goes about having a very interesting and destructive day. The city, despite its beautiful and mild climate, has been turned into an urban nightmare by the misdeeds and bad thoughts of humanity. Gang members try to kill him, but he gets one of their guns and shoots his would-be assassin in the leg, saying, "That's the concept. Take some shooting lessons, asshole." Later, our hero is shocked, genuinely shocked, to realize that, in the end, he has become the bad guy.

Someone holds a sign: "We're dying of AIDS please help us." Another sign: "Will work for food." He meets a neo-Nazi who has a can of Zyklon B in his antique store (the poison used to kill the Jews in the Nazi death camps). At one point, Douglas looks through a hole in his shoe, at the smog hanging over the city. Even nature is getting destroyed by this place.

With such thoughts in mind, it's no surprise that Los Angeles is also a go-to location for depictions of *future* awfulness—from the mildly disturbing *Her* (2013), in which a man falls in love with his operating system, to *Blade Runner* (1982) and *Hotel Artemis* (2018). But to nail down fully Los Angeles's identification with the awful present, let's look at the contrast between *Saturday Night Fever* (1977) and *Grease* (1978), both starring John Travolta and released within six months of each other.

One seems tough, but it's soft. (Of course, that's the New York film.) One seems soft, but it's hard. (Of course, that's the

Los Angeles film.) Both have a lot in common, but in terms of message, they are mirror opposites.

Saturday Night Fever is set in the Bay Ridge section of Brooklyn, and it's all about disco and the disco ethos. Tony Manero (Travolta) works in a paint store and by night he's king of the dance floor. He loves dancing—it's the only pure thing in his life. Otherwise, everything's pretty ugly, and he's part of the ugliness. He lives in a racist, sexist environment, and everyone he knows is a moron, including the guy he sees in the mirror. The movie glorifies Tony's moments on the dance floor—he really does have a gift, and the scenes of him performing carry a sense of the splendor of this disco world and era. But the movie overall does not endorse the disco mentality.

In that sense, *Saturday Night Fever* details a moral journey. For a dance contest, Tony teams up with a partner, a slightly older woman who lives in Manhattan and aspires to a life of refinement. She's not nearly arrived, but she is several steps ahead of Tony. Eventually, the two compete in the contest and win, but Tony knows that the deck was stacked. They should have lost to a Puerto Rican couple, and they would have were it not for racism. This makes the victory worse than meaningless to Tony—it threatens to corrupt the only thing about himself and his world that he actually loves.

Later that night, he sits in the front seat of a car as a nice girl he knows is gang-raped in the back. Oh, and a friend falls to his death from the Verrazzano Bridge. So taken together, it's an instructive evening, the kind dramatic enough to get even an idiot's attention. Tony witnesses the consequences of racism, sexism, brutality, and epic stupidity, and after a long subway ride, he concludes that he would like a life that's not racist, sexist, brutal, or stupid. Basically, he wants to be an artist.

Now, in a sense, *Saturday Night Fever* tries to have it both ways, because viewers do leave the movie remembering the gloriousness of Tony on the dance floor. Nonetheless, the movie accurately depicts the ethos at the heart of the disco mentality of the day—and rejects it entirely. This makes the movie surprisingly complex and humane for something built to sell a soundtrack.

Now, let's look at *Grease*. It's ostensibly a movie about the 1950s. It's set in 1958/59, and it's based on a musical that was set at the same time. But something happened between the musical's debut in 1971 and its transformation into a movie some seven years later. Disco happened. And so *Grease* is a weird hybrid, a movie that's supposedly set in the 1950s but that celebrates the connection between the 1950s greaser mentality and the mentality of the sexist goons like Tony Manero's friends in *Saturday Night Fever*. The connection is amplified by the fact that the two movies star the same actor, John Travolta. And the title song "Grease" was written by Barry Gibb of the Bee Gees, who wrote the soundtrack to *Saturday Night Fever*.

The movie is the story of Danny (Travolta) and Sandy (Olivia Newton-John), who meet and fall in love during the summer, but in the fall, when they find themselves at the same high school, their friends get in the way. He has an image of himself as a tough guy, so he deliberately acts indifferent toward her, and she, being rather sweet and naive, gets confused and put off. But never fear. After lots of side stories and various complications, we get the "happy" ending, in which Sandy shows up with a bad perm, decked out in black leather and spiked heels, and smoking a cigarette. He loves it; they sing a song, and everybody's delighted.

But they shouldn't be, because if you think about it, *Grease* is a depressing story. Sandy starts off as a genuine, spontaneous young woman. She and Danny establish a rapport. But then, because of the brutal stupidity of their environment, they both feel they have to adopt these rigid and unfulfilling sex roles. This results, ultimately, in her turning herself into an objectified siren and denying her own nature, just for this clown. And the movie presents all this as a victory.

This is a more subtle version of Los Angeles being the setting for modern awfulness. L.A. is never mentioned—the movie is just located there. The year, 1978, is never mentioned—the pretense is that it's set in an earlier time. Yet the movie was directly in conversation with the young people of its era about the then-current ethos. It was a direct refutation of the humane ending of *Saturday Night Fever*—an embrace of the very sexist attitudes that the earlier film had rejected six months before.

In *Saturday Night Fever*, a man ultimately realizes he must become some variety of sensitive human being. In *Grease*, a woman realizes that she must stop being a sensitive human being, and the whole audience is expected to laugh and cheer and celebrate as another one bites the dust.

What's that, you say? *Grease* isn't *really* a Los Angeles film. That's a point of view, and I understand it. Still, it's difficult to imagine *Grease* turning out the same had it been filmed in New York, Chicago, or San Francisco. It would never have turned out so hard.

CHAPTER FIVE
Junk Food for the Soul

America is the land of immigrants, but for most families, the immigration thing happened a long time ago. California is a nation of *recent* immigrants, some from other countries, some from other states in the Union. Their friends stayed home. California is for people who said, "No, I don't like what life is giving me, and I'm willing to try something else." Yes, California does indeed have people who were actually born here, including Native people whose roots in the area go back thousands of years. But it remains, as powerfully as ever, a beacon and a lure that goes right across the country.

If you say the name "Montana" or "Wisconsin" or "Oklahoma," these places will mean something to anyone in the United States, and they may conjure up images or facts or history. But California, like New York City, and perhaps nowhere else in the entire country, presents every American mind with something whole and beyond that. Like New York, California is a moral concept. It is something that everyone in America must make a decision about, according to his or her own values, knowledge, or lack thereof.

No one who hasn't been to Nebraska has any particular idea about Nebraska that goes beyond some pictures or guesses involving corn, or snow, or tornadoes. But everyone in the United States decides how they *feel* about California. And the feelings can be anything, based on any number of facts, real or imagined, that a person chooses to believe. California is large. It contains multitudes, and so virtually anything you think about it will be, at least to some extent, true, unless you think it's small and doesn't matter.

Mostly, the feelings about California will be ones of either approval or disapproval. To most of America, California is either good or bad.

Some people want to move here and will. Some people want to move here, but know they never will, but are okay with California as a kind of dream or idea. And some people aren't interested—they're quite happy where they are. But in that last category, there are still others who, despite not wanting to live here, feel the presence of California as some alternate possibility, not only in American life, but within their own consciousness— an open door that they can choose to go through or not, but whose existence they resent and wish they could ignore.

Curiously, this last category also contains people who make generalizations about how we in California feel about *them*, when people in California aren't thinking of them at all, beyond a vague wishing them well. We can't quite imagine them, simply because, for better or worse and probably mostly for better, there is no national mythology surrounding their location. We do notice, when we go to the middle of the country, that the people tend to be friendlier, and fatter, and with an unaccountable tendency to be politically bizarre, but these are just impressions, hardly fully formed opinions.

We also notice, when we travel to other places in the United States, that we meet people who love to tell us all about California, to fill us in about little details, about how the whole state is going broke, or how this or that congresswoman's district is a disaster. But when we ask them when was the last time they were in California, they usually say they were never there. But they know all about it. From a friend. Who probably has also never been there.

IF AMERICA IS WHERE EUROPEANS WENT in order to practice their religion, California is the place where Americans came to lose theirs—or at least to lose constraint. They also saw California as a land of plenty, where excess was possible. It overflowed with bounty.

The first impetus for major migration to California was not freedom or the prospect of all-night parties but the Gold Rush— that is, money, that which makes freedom and parties possible. This event, which vibrated across the continent, made California a state and brought into the American consciousness and most particularly and strongly into the California consciousness, the idea that a sudden change in fortune is possible, and that that's the best thing you could hope for in life. You just need to hit the right rock with the right pick. Or go to the right party and charm the right bigshot. Then you're made.

Europe is about old money. The East Coast is about new money pretending to be old money. California is about new money getting thrown around, and it has been that way forever. It was about the new millionaire going on a spree in old San Francisco, and about newly minted movie stars driving down Hollywood Boulevard in a Hispano Suiza convertible with a tiger in the front seat. And now it's about dot.com billionaires rattling their upscale neighbors with repulsive reconstruction projects. It's the place for showing off.

But because it is also a place almost defined by its lack of tradition, by the non-influence of family, and by the absence of religion as the ultimate defining value, there's a disconnectedness at the heart of California life. Everyone is remaking themselves, but everyone is starting from scratch, and that's a recipe for loneliness, doubt, and despair. Even for the most successful and privileged, there's a sense of reaching a dead-end at the ocean's edge.

It's a funny thing about paradise. If you are in a beautiful place, and the weather is great, and every day is fun, and you lack for nothing, and every need is met and every desire is answered and realized, then there's only one thing left to worry about— death, only the biggest thing of all.

The guy who is worried about catching the bus and if the boss is in a good mood, is not worried about anything big, because small things have rented out his mind. But when you're standing there with nothing but time and nothing between you and the sea and sky, the real problems of life come into focus. This is the irony and dilemma of mortals in paradise.

Yet belief in something higher is intrinsic to human happiness and to the structure of the human psyche. And so higher things end up being manufactured, one way or the other, by synthetic means. Thus, California becomes the manufacturing center for an endless series of nouveau quasi-religious cults, churning out false idols for collective worship; that is, the movie business.

TWO CALIFORNIA MEMORIES.

The first: I was in Los Angeles because a production company was making a documentary out of my first book. Of course, I was happy about this, but I was even happier because I'd just been told that day that I was going to be given an Associate Producer credit in the documentary. Now, as anyone knows, Associate Producer in Hollywood is the equivalent of Commendatore in Italy: It means absolutely nothing, but come on—it *sounds amazing.*

That night, I was driving down Wilshire Boulevard in my rental car. For once, there was no traffic. I had the radio on— Madonna's "Beautiful Stranger" was playing—and a feeling came over me. If you've ever been to Southern California, you know that feeling. It's the one where the world is beautiful, the air is warm, and the future is glowing. You have no cares, but you have lots of things to do. It's not exactly a feeling of being in love with life. No, it's much better than that. It's a feeling of life being in love with *you.* And on this occasion, part of that feeling—not the biggest part, but in there with the palm trees and the warm, rushing air—had to do with the completely baseless thought that I was now a Hollywood producer, a thought that, in the very moment of enjoying it, I knew wasn't really true.

Thus, it was a moment of real happiness brought on by a

superficial response to a conscious illusion. But knowing it was illusory and knowing I was being superficial didn't make the happiness any less real. It just made it very, *very* California.

Now the second story: Again, I was in Los Angeles, this time in my capacity as a journalist. I had to interview somebody for some movie or other, I don't remember who or what for. Most people think interviewing famous people is a great way to meet them, but it's the worst, full of all kinds of unpleasant power dynamics, where you try to get them to say something new, and they try to feed you some predigested party line. It's not fun, which explains why I don't remember why I was there. Such memories tend to be repressed.

In any case, on this particular evening, I'd finished work for the day. I saw what looked like a nice restaurant, so I walked inside to get some dinner. As soon as I did, I could feel a certain— not tension, but elevation in the air. It was palpable, enough so that it took only a few seconds for me to recognize the source of this elevation and turn in its direction. Morgan Freeman was standing at the bar. He wore a tan leather jacket and aside from being a little taller than I expected, he looked exactly like Morgan Freeman, just standing there, talking to whoever talked to him.

He was not bothering anybody. Except he was bothering *everybody*. Just by being there, he became the organizing principle for every other element in that room. He became the sun, and everything else was a satellite, some of us planets, some of us dead moons, either embracing the sun's presence or unwittingly and unwillingly reflecting its light. And it was a strange and depressing thing for all of us. It was almost certainly depressing for Freeman himself, in that it was clearly impossible for this man ever to go to a normal place, have a normal drink, and feel normal about it. On the contrary, this was his fate, to walk into rooms and *disturb* them, to wreck his own time and everyone else's. Yet the situation was infinitely more depressing for everyone *else* in that room, every one of whom got a forced lesson in their own comparative unimportance.

This is the flipside of superficial California values, the price we pay for those rare and elusive feelings of counterfeit euphoria. The air is forcibly pumped out of the pumped-up ego, and we're left with no stronger values to counter this valuation of self in terms of fame, money, power, and success.

IN 1989, CHRISTOPHER GUEST released a film called *The Big Picture*, which did absolutely nothing at the time of its release—it grossed about $100,000—but has gained a certain life on video and seems on the way to being regarded as a minor classic. It stars Kevin Bacon as a young guy, just out of film school, who gets a development deal and a small amount of money and immediately goes Hollywood in a bad way.

At the start of the film, he has a best friend, who is a burgeoning cinematographer (Michael McKean), and a lovely and supportive girlfriend (Emily Longstreth), but at the first whisper of possible success, he alienates both of them. He breaks up with the girlfriend because a beautiful TV actress (Teri Hatcher) seems to take an interest in him, and he agrees to work with a major cinematographer without once mentioning to his producer that he'd planned to use his friend as the cameraman. He gives up the people closest to him without a fight, without even a stray impulse to do otherwise.

He gives up his artistic integrity as well, also without a fight. He has an idea to make a movie about two men and a woman, all in their forties, snowed in at a cabin in New England—a chamber drama, in which it's revealed the woman, who is married to one of the men, had an affair with the other. The producer's idea is to make the characters much younger and to change the cast to two women and one man and to add a lesbian element. And that's just the first of the compromises. Soon, our hero is agreeing to a wall-to-wall soundtrack of popular hits and a change in setting, from winter to summer.

This path, of course, leads to disaster. The project blows up, and he's left with nothing—no best friend, no girlfriend, no TV star, no Porsche, no nothing except a low-end job and the shame of having revealed his shallowness to everyone, including himself. This sets the stage for his redemption: He does a rock video that gets spotted in Hollywood and then—most crucially (and hard to believe)—he puts off taking a call from a producer, thus creating (by accident) a false perception that he's in demand.

The point here seems to be that so much of Hollywood success depends on luck that one might as well choose today as the day to have integrity—first, because there might not be another chance to have it, and second, because integrity is so original it just might work as a strategy. And if it doesn't, at least you haven't disgraced yourself by turning into a Hollywood cliché.

All this makes *The Big Picture* about what one might expect in terms of message and story. But there are other elements that complicate the message and reveal a more sophisticated examination of the California dream. It's notable, for example, that Kevin Bacon remains throughout a sympathetic figure. Even at his worst, when he's gone Hollywood to the extent that he's mistreating his closest friend, we are enlisted into his corruption. We wish he would behave otherwise, but we understand the allure of what he's experiencing.

At one point in the film, he is driving down the highway on a sunny day. Having left his girlfriend, he is on his way to the beautiful TV star's house, filled with self-satisfaction and dreams of guaranteed sex and success (so he believes). In this moment, he is a free man, a man released into the easiness and joy of superficiality, living in the world of ego and breathing the pure air of nothing but fun. No one watching will have any trouble understanding how he feels and why he feels that way. The desire to be free is largely the desire to shed responsibility and the requirements of seriousness, and who wouldn't want to do that, at least for a time?

Something else, too: The screenplay is wise in making Kevin Bacon's dream movie, the one he wants to make, seem awful. Three people in their forties stuck in a cabin talking about their relationship sounds like one of those dull Ingmar Bergman-inspired Woody Allen dramas from the same era, the ones that nobody wanted to see, not then or since. And though the original premise for the film is eventually distorted beyond recognition —in one iteration, it's set in a sorority—the first producer's initial idea sounds a lot more appealing: A young husband and wife go to a remote cabin with a woman friend, and it's revealed that the two *women* had an affair. I'd much rather watch that movie than the one Kevin Bacon starts off wanting to make.

In this instance, too, *The Big Picture* enlists us in an illicit complicity, this time with the producer, but in each case with what might be called superficial Hollywood values. Anyone who sees the film remembers Martin Short as Kevin Bacon's agent. He's an outlandish, absurd figure, full of false assurances and meaningless friendliness, an East Coast person's fantasy of bizarre California behavior. What it takes an extra viewing or two to realize is that, for all his ridiculousness, *he's actually a really good agent.* At every turn, he gives his client strategically smart advice.

These Hollywood hands know something about human beings, something that the young filmmaker is discovering about himself: *This is what people are like.* The superficial is what most people want, in their lives and their entertainment. Thus, in the Hollywood context, maintaining one's integrity is not just difficult but beside the point. It's like holding a torch for values that don't quite exist.

THE STANDARD WAY OF THINKING about movies is to assume that Hollywood offers entertainment to distract people from their troubles. But what if it does the opposite? Perhaps what it really does is distract us from our *lack* of troubles, so as to distract us from our one real trouble, which is mortality. We go to the movies trouble-free and become engrossed in the fictional troubles of other people, so as not to look inside and face the only trouble to be had in a world of plenty, the prospect of someday leaving it.

In this way, Hollywood is a massive factory designed to generate and promote all that is unreal and unimportant in the grand scheme, because the reality is that most people would rather avoid the grand scheme for as long as possible.

There's a wonderful moment at the end of *Valley Girl* (1983), mysterious in its beauty. The whole movie is about the cultural divide between the well-off Valley Girl (Deborah Foreman) and the kid from the wrong side of the tracks, the punk rocker, played by Nicolas Cage. In the end, all the obstacles to their relationship have been resolved, and in the last shot of the film, as they ride in a limousine, you see, outside the car window, a shot of the Sherman Oaks Galleria, all lit up and inviting.

That sign invites us to come to the mall; that this is a place of beauty and splendor, this is a place of dreams, this is a wonderful place where people are happy and buy things. And Los Angeles County is a place where such places exist—promising comfort and realization of aspiration—where youth is forever and love stories are always happening.

Yes, you could say it's just a mall. But you might as well say, "It's only a movie." After all, it's not the thing itself but the access that thing has to the spirit. It's a vision of nourishing emptiness, of junk food for the soul. But if the junk food supply is endless, you will never starve.

HOWEVER, YOU MIGHT FEEL SICK, AFTER A WHILE.

In the early 1990s, screenwriter Michael Tolkin addressed these concerns directly with a series of films that expressed the dead-end of consumption and the hunger for something more: *The Rapture* (1991), which he wrote and directed; *The Player* (1992), which he wrote, adapting his own novel; *Deep Cover* (1992), which he cowrote, based on his own story; and *The New Age* (1994), which he wrote and directed. With sophistication, with humor, and with some alarm, all the films, each in a different way, examine the soul-sickness at the heart of Southern California values.

The most ambitious of these was *The Rapture*, with Mimi Rogers as a woman in a monotonous, soul-killing job and whose entire personal life is devoted to sexual pleasure. By day, she works as an information operator. By night, she and a somewhat older European man, Vic (Patrick Bauchau), cruise nightclubs looking for swinging couples. In an early scene, Rogers sits on the roof of a convertible, at the start of a warm California night, discussing where they might go. Perhaps a hotel near the airport? She looks free—it's the start of the weekend—and we're confronted with a vision of someone basking in the happiness of emptiness. And we're with her, feeling her sense of anticipation, for unknown thrills just minutes or hours away.

But it turns out that Sharon (Rogers) is not the kind of sensualist who can be content forever with the sensual. Her hedonism is all about wanting to transcend her experience, to find something bigger than herself, and so she is becoming disenchanted with this go-nowhere way of life. This disenchantment is forming just as she overhears people at work talking about experiencing visions indicating the imminence of the Rapture, in which the righteous will be instantly lifted up into heaven, just in time to miss the tribulation leading up to Armageddon.

Tolkin's screenplay takes as a given the dead-on accuracy of Christian cosmology and then shows what would happen— how people would react—if every bit of it were true. Sharon gets religion, marries, has a daughter, and seems on the way to having a tranquil yet purposeful life. But after the husband is killed in a workplace shooting, she starts to become unhinged. She has a vision that tells her to go into the desert with her daughter and await the Rapture, but it's implied that the vision might actually be from the devil. And then in an act of colossal perversity—for which she can never forgive herself, nor forgive God for not stopping her—she kills her own daughter, in order to send her soul to heaven.

The idea here seems to be that even if it's all true, and a person knows the correct path, the spiritual hazards are still enormous; and that a personality that takes devotion to excess—whether to sensuality or religion—is especially prone to disaster. The movie might also be saying that the vision was not from the devil but from God, that the universe is a little more casual and less organized than we'd like to think.

In any case, it's hard to imagine a movie presenting modern life and one woman's reaction against it being quite as effective were it set in any city besides Los Angeles.

Along the same line we find *The Player*, in which screenwriter Tolkin and director Robert Altman give us characters who experience no redemption, and who constantly choose self-interest and indifference to the suffering of others and are rewarded for it. The movie is beyond caustic in its view of the Hollywood ethos. It depicts active spiritual malice as a requisite for success in being a studio head. The main character, played by Tim Robbins, kills someone, covers up the crime, coldly and publicly rejects his own kind and devoted girlfriend, and then in the heat of passion, he confesses his murder to his new lover, the girlfriend of the dead man. She is unfazed, and the two go on having a happy and successful life, one of power and wealth and a baby on the way.

Deep Cover, unlike the other two films, is a crime movie, but it plays in the same spiritual terrain. Laurence Fishburne is a Los Angeles detective who goes deep undercover, so deep that he becomes a drug kingpin and is enjoying the lifestyle. His associate is Jeff Goldblum, a lawyer from the suburbs who gets into the drug business out of some twist in his psyche that makes him want more and more. "I want my cake and eat it, too," he says, almost as if in a trance—entranced by the desire to acquire.

The movie is all about the drive to be more than you are—which is at the heart of all California movies, from *The Wizard of Oz* through *Once Upon a Time . . . in Hollywood*. It's about losing yourself in a way of life that is, at once, seductive and superficial; that feeds most needs but not ultimate needs; and like *The Player*, it's about pursuing that life and those desires while surrounded by people who want what they want as much as you want what you want but may be willing to fight harder and care less for the niceties of human interaction than you do. It's about being in a business that sells superficiality, that rewards superficiality, that offers superficial (but undeniable) pleasure in reward; and so it can't be surprising that the kind of people who are attracted to the business aren't necessarily deep, or nice.

Tolkin's final distillation of these ideas comes with *The New Age*, a box office disaster in its time (it grossed only $245K and played in only two theaters). The essential problem for audiences of the time was the movie's strange straddling of the line between seriousness and satire, which probably left them unsure as to how to receive the film. In retrospect, the tone makes sense, in that Tolkin correctly captures a world that is a borderline satire of itself.

The film is the story of a married couple that has the accoutrements of wealth, but no security. They have a big house with a big pool—the obligatory staging for that other staple of Hollywood mythmaking, the Hollywood party. But the marriage is joyless. The wife (Judy Davis) is insecure. The husband (Peter Weller) is cheating. Both are miserable, but in that odd state of misery where they imagine themselves at the very least enviable, and so they have the satisfaction of residual pride. Then the husband, in a colossal act of self-sabotage, quits his $300K-a-year studio job in search of something more fulfilling, and the couple enter a slow and tumultuous spiral.

They get into New Age spiritualism, which is presented as a combination of charlatanism and solipsism, in which nonsense is presented as irrefutable truth and penetrating observation. They are yet another illustration of the trap that lies in wait for those who believe in nothing—they're likely to believe in anything.

In Tolkin's films we get a portrait of Southern California as a spiritual wasteland—that's nothing new. What's new is the idea that the wasteland both inadequately attends to and aggravates the search for something deeper. Meanwhile, contact with the guiding inner voice is lost in the clamor of sensation, to the point that all that's wanted is that elusive cake that stays whole even as it's eaten.

YET THERE IS ONE CONSISTENT SOURCE of rebuttal to this depiction of California as a place of ultimate spiritual desolation. The rebuttal can be found in the California films that deal with the Latinx experience. That this should be the case is especially understandable when we consider films such as *El Norte* (1983) and *Under the Same Moon* (2007), in which the characters, in some cases as a matter of survival, expend great effort to cross the American border. In such contexts, the America of California would be perceived as a land of deliverance.

But this optimism can also be found in films depicting characters who possess a realistic grasp of American racism and prejudice, as well as of the simple difficulties of arriving in a country with absolutely no power or connections. *Stand and Deliver* (1988) tells the story of Jaime Escalante, a high school math teacher who inspired his students to excel in calculus. In the film, the students do so well that the Educational Testing Service assumes they cheated. Obviously, in that assumption, there is an element of what George W. Bush once called "the soft bigotry of low expectations." But the overall message that comes through is that, with tenacity and a certain acquired imperviousness, any success is possible.

Perhaps what keeps these Latinx films from degenerating into cynicism is that the characters usually don't fully embrace the values of the California culture. Yes, they aspire to material prosperity, but they stay grounded, to a healthy extent, in the values of family. The unsung epic *Mi Familia* (1995) shows a single family over the course of fifty years and three generations. It presents an America that is harsh on Mexican immigrants, even legal ones. Early in the film, a young pregnant woman (Jennifer Lopez) destined to become the family matriarch is deported in a routine roundup, even though she's an American citizen. Throughout, more terrible things happen to her family members. Some are calamities of their own making, and some are exacerbated by unfair or unfeeling authorities. Yet by the end, when the founding couple looks back with satisfaction at their lives, the audience is invited to share in that satisfaction. Something in the alchemy of the family's traditional ways, in combination with their adopted country's opportunities, has made for a hard yet good life.

Patricia Cardoso's *Real Women Have Curves* (2002) explores family, but from a different angle, with America Ferrera as Ana, an exceptional student with a full scholarship to Columbia, whose family seems determined to kill her dreams. Her mother wants her to stay in East Los Angeles and work in a dress factory. Mom seems to have internalized none of the positive aspects of the United States, but she *has* internalized the dominant culture's love of thinness, and so she fat-shames her daughter at every opportunity. In the best-known scene from the film, Ana rebels and invites a factory floor of plus-sized women to get relief from the heat by stripping down to their underwear. She rebels yet again by accepting the scholarship, and the last moments show Ana walking confidently down a street in New York City.

Would it have been the same movie had Ana ended up at Stanford, not Columbia? Aside from the visual impact of New York versus Palo Alto, it might have been too much of a stretch to express such unalloyed optimism in a California setting. Unlike New York, where everything's on the surface, there's usually something scary at the end of a California rainbow.

CHAPTER SIX

Hollywood and Pearl Harbor

Once upon a time, California was very far away, a vast expanse at the end of another even vaster expanse, which was the United States. Today we live with two heavily populated coasts and with an enormous but less populated "flyover" area in between, but this was not the case in the first decades of the twentieth century. Even by then, the western migration had not fully taken hold.

Instead, there was the East Coast and there was the densely populated industrial Midwest, and then there was that whole area west of Illinois that most people never visited and not many people lived in. California had two major population centers then, San Francisco and Los Angeles. They were bona fide big cities, while San Diego was comparatively small and San Jose was little bigger than a town. Most of the state was farmland. In the 1920 presidential election, California commanded thirteen electoral votes—fewer than New Jersey, though California is more than twenty times larger than New Jersey in area. California had lots of empty space.

In the early days of Hollywood, when filmmakers such as

Charles Chaplin and Buster Keaton would take their cameras out into the street, they ended up capturing Los Angeles and its environs circa 1920. In those films, we see that empty space, even in the city itself. The streets are wide. The buildings have lots of room to breathe. It's the urban equivalent of looking at a gangly thirteen-year-old, one that you can tell already is going to be very tall. Everything about Los Angeles, every corner, every intersection, every vista and streetcar, suggests potential.

When people around the country thought of the state during this period, they thought of oranges. They might have also thought of earthquakes and movies, and, even then, they might have thought of newfangled crackpot ideas, but when they *pictured* the state, when they put an image in their head, it was of an orange grove. Rows and rows of orange groves—to infinity.

In 1934, W. C. Fields made his funniest comedy, *It's a Gift*, about a grocer in the middle of the country who has a California dream. He takes his modest inheritance, from a recently deceased relative, and buys an orange grove. He wants that dream. The dream turns out a little different than he expects, but he makes out all right, the reward of all those—at least all those in movies— who try.

Honestly, I don't think it's even possible for us to arrange our minds to imagine how blessedly disconnected California must have felt for the people who lived here one hundred years ago. I can only say, from my own experience, that even in the mid-1980s it felt much farther away from the East Coast than it does now. There was television, but there was no Internet, and thus no instant interconnectivity of ideas. It really felt, in a way that perhaps can't fully be conveyed, that we were our own thing.

California remained something of a backwater for years and years. And then the war came—a war so big that it was simply called "the war" for the rest of the twentieth century. World War II transformed California into an economic powerhouse. It also became a debarkation point for thousands upon thousands of soldiers heading into the Pacific theater of the conflict. Soldiers from all over the country finally got to see it, this place they would otherwise never have seen. And as any nonagenarian can tell you, what they thought was, "Okay. If I survive this war, I'm not going back to Oshkosh. If I come back alive, I'm going to *stay* alive in *this* gorgeous place."

World War II turned out to be the best advertisement for California that anyone could ever have imagined. But that's how things *turned out*. World War II started in sheer terror, and this terror is reflected in the movies that were made in and set in California during the months following the disaster at Pearl Harbor. These are not the World War II movies that we remember today. They're not ones we're all that proud of. Our collective memory is of war films without blood but with lots of patriotism, and featuring jolly platoons populated by stereotypical rednecks from Alabama, Jews from New York, and a few scattered Italians from New York or Philadelphia, usually with a WASP as the commanding officer.

But in the immediate aftermath of Pearl Harbor, movie studios were producing something else, films reflecting a country that was fearful and paranoid, full of hatred and suspicion, and understandably fixated on possible sabotage, espionage, and invasion.

That the racial disturbances toward people of Asian descent

got very bad indeed has been the subject of many books, and this can't be one of them. This is a book about movies. But still, it might be instructive and helpful to look at the state of play for Asians in American cinema in the years before the attack on Pearl Harbor.

WHAT MAKES THE EARLY HOLLYWOOD treatment of Asian people so interesting, bizarre, and confounding is that it reveals such a mix of influences and impulses, both positive and negative. The treatment of African Americans was different—it was mostly condescending and demeaning, with some positive portrayals here and there, but with no real possibilities for any African American actor to achieve stardom. Asians in Hollywood, by contrast, could become famous, although often only by playing stereotypes of Asian exoticism. And even for those who managed to have successful careers, there was still a major obstacle. When the very best Asian roles came along, they'd usually be cast with white actors.

The Japanese actor Sessue Hayakawa became a matinee idol in the early silent era, but usually for playing villains. The Chinese American actress Anna May Wong became famous in later silent films but became so frustrated by the roles she was getting in Hollywood that she left to pursue a career in London. Wong's move was rather like what the African American dancer and actress Josephine Baker did around the same time, only she went to Paris. But unlike Baker, Wong came back and resumed her Hollywood career, starring in movies such as *Daughter of the Dragon* (1931), in which she played a princess who teams up with her long-lost father, the evil Dr. Fu Manchu, played by the Swedish actor Warner Oland. She had perhaps her best showcase—and certainly her most enduring one—in a supporting role in the Josef von Sternberg/Marlene Dietrich classic *Shanghai Express* (1932), as a Chinese prostitute who kills an evil warlord, played, again, by Oland.

Wong had the makings of A-list stardom. She was beautiful and had an unexpectedly low voice, ideal for the talkies. But her career was mostly one of frustration. In 1937, she hoped to play O-Lan in the MGM production of *The Good Earth*, but the role went to German actress Luise Rainer, who won an Oscar for her performance. As if for the unwitting double crime of taking the role that should have been Wong's and also taking the Oscar that should have been Greta Garbo's (for *Camille*) the year before, Rainer's career quickly unraveled, but Wong kept working, in films and television, until her death in 1961.

The main obstacle to Wong's career was Hollywood's unwillingness to present an interracial love scene on screen. In 1932, an actress could not be a major star without appearing in love stories, but Wong wasn't allowed to star opposite Clark Gable or Robert Montgomery or Gary Cooper. In fact, one of the main reasons Wong wasn't cast in *The Good Earth* was because MGM wanted Paul Muni, a white actor, to play O-Lan's husband. Even a love scene between an Asian actress and a white actor in yellowface would have been considered unacceptable. The only way Wong could have starred in a love story would have been opposite another Asian actor, and in the Hollywood of the 1920s and '30s, there were no male Asian movie stars.

The Bitter Tea of General Yen (1933) is a great film from Frank Capra and a complicated entry in the annals of yellowface on screen, in that its message was subversive and it pushed at the boundaries of its era. The film took place in China and starred Nils Asther, a 6'1" Swedish actor, to play a Chinese warlord. Over the course of the film, an American missionary (Barbara Stanwyck) is rescued by Yen and comes under his protection in his palace. She thinks of him as a heathen, but the whole point of the film is that she has a lot to learn from *him*, and, by extension, the West has much to learn from the East. She becomes attracted to him, and the two even kiss in a dream sequence, a daring move in that, even though Asther and Stanwyck were both white, they were depicting interracial love. Ultimately, the idea here is that she has been enlightened and erotically awakened through her contact with this man.

Other films starring white actors as Asian characters were more bizarre, such as *The Hatchet Man* and *The Son-Daughter*, both from 1932 and both set in San Francisco's Chinatown. The former starred Edward G. Robinson as the assassin for a tong, or Chinese gang, and the latter starred Helen Hayes and Ramon Novarro as would-be lovers whose lives are disrupted by violence and conflicting political allegiances within their community. The portrayals are sympathetic and even positive, but the spectacle of Robinson and Loretta Young disguised as Chinese characters, and Ramon Novarro bald except for a long cue, seems weird and absurd. Likewise, the repeated emphasis on exoticism and violence, which we see in many Asian-themed films from this period, seems like willful insistence by the majority culture to see a race of people in a particular, stereotyped, and limited way.

In these portrayals, Asian characters simply weren't treated as "real" in the same way white characters were.

Charlie Chan and Mr. Moto—fictional Chinese and Japanese detectives, respectively—were the protagonists of a series of films in which they were played by white actors. They were heroes, in a sense—sly, elusive, and highly intelligent. Those very same positive qualities, which were cultural assumptions about Asians in general, easily turned negative when the rest of the country felt threatened. Sly and intelligent became sneaky and dangerous in the Hollywood imagination of 1942.

THE DAY AFTER THE JAPANESE ATTACK on Pearl Harbor, President Franklin Roosevelt called it "a day that will live in infamy," but it hasn't lived in infamy. Though it was disaster and a calamity, Pearl Harbor has instead lived in American memory as the opening chapter in a book of strife and sacrifice that, at least for the United States, ended well. In less than four years, the United States emerged as the strongest military and economic power in the world. Pearl Harbor has rather gone into legend as a powerful sucker punch, after which the country got up from the mat and won.

For this reason, it takes a real act of the imagination to cast one's mind back to the sense of impotence and uncertainty following the attack, a period that few alive today can remember firsthand. It was close to sheer terror. Mayor Fiorello La Guardia of New York City went on the radio to tell his constituents how to prepare for an aerial attack, and there were reports of Nazi submarines coming into American coastal waters. There was every expectation that our coastal cities, like those in Europe, were about to be bombed.

As was the case following 9/11, there was both the sense that everything had changed and the fear that worse was still to come. But unlike 9/11, the lives of everyone in the country *did* change—immediately—and terrible things *did* come, albeit not on American shores. The private plans of millions were put on hold and discarded. Normal citizens who'd been minding their own business suddenly had to get married right away or not married at all; they had to leave school and leave their families. They had to work in plants. They had to use ration cards and not buy a new car, because the country wasn't making new cars, just jeeps and trucks for the military. The awfulness of 9/11 changed the national consciousness, but the Pearl Harbor effect was more tangible. It was the attack that kept on attacking, touching the lives of every single person in the country in ways big and small, and all of them bad.

Panic, rage, and a determination to do something in response flooded the country after Pearl Harbor, but nowhere was the panic more intense than on the West Coast, where the fear and expectation was that Japan might attack any minute. Such was the terror that there was even the fear—one which probably had no basis in reality—that Japan might land an occupying force in San Francisco or Los Angeles.

Even with the instructive comparison to 9/11, it's still hard to bring back the intensity of those emotions, and for that reason, the movies of the time become useful as historical documents. It took a few years for Hollywood to dramatize the 9/11 attacks, but the Pearl Harbor debacle took place in the era of the big studios, with their vast machinery already in place. Just as the country was able to mobilize its industrial might for war purposes, Hollywood went into instant overdrive for movie purposes. Scripts were written in days, and productions went before the cameras within the month. Throughout 1942—the most difficult year of the war from the Allied perspective—the movies kept coming, filling the minds of viewers like the nightmares of a patient suffering from post-traumatic stress.

One of the running motifs was that there were secret societies of fifth columnists planning the overthrow of the United States. (Sometimes, as though participating in satanic rituals, they even wore hoods and robes, as they did in the Bowery Boys film *Let's Get Tough!* from July of 1942.) Tiny Monogram Pictures got out the first anti-Japan film, a spy thriller in which plastic surgeons transform Japanese agents so they look like American government officials. It was released in March.

Secret Agent of Japan, released by 20th Century-Fox, was the first anti-Japanese movie from a major studio. The earliest draft dates from December 10, 1941, though some press reports suggest that the scenario might have been prepared earlier, with the likelihood of war in mind. Like many films of this intense early period of the war, it deals with an unsuccessful effort by the Americans to penetrate a Japanese spy ring—a spy ring that is, ultimately, defeated, but not before the Pearl Harbor attack. Over and over in these films, the motif plays out like an anxiety dream, in which Americans keep *almost* stopping the attack, without success.

The film was set in Shanghai, but filmed in Los Angeles, and the circumstances of the filming are even more notable than the film itself. Thirty Japanese American actors appeared in it, all of them American citizens, and before being cast, they were subject to investigation by the FBI and Naval Intelligence. They weren't *told* they were being investigated, they just had photographic tests made with the film's star, Lynn Bari, and the footage was passed on to government officials. Four policeman, uniformed and plain-clothed, were on the set at all times, and the Japanese American actors weren't allowed to leave the set unless accompanied by one of them. This was supposedly done for two reasons: To prevent the actors from being attacked and, according to a press release, "to prevent studio employees from becoming used to the sight of Japanese soldiers in case the real thing should someday appear."

That's how weak and worried people in Los Angeles felt at the start of the war. They not only thought it possible that the Japanese would launch a ground attack, but they worried that the sight of Japanese soldiers might become a familiar one on Los Angeles streets.

Secret Agent of Japan was released in April. In May, Republic Pictures released *Remember Pearl Harbor*. Planning for that film began on December 16, 1941, with the intention of its being the first film dealing with the Pearl Harbor attack. Filmed partly in Redondo Beach, but set in the Philippines, it tells a convoluted story of carefree, unsuspecting Americans stumbling across Nazi spies who are coordinating with the Japanese military and providing critical aid for the sneak attack. The film, which uses actual footage from Pearl Harbor, ends with Japanese soldiers landing in the Philippines and with the hero flying a suicide mission—piloting a plane into a Japanese aircraft carrier. An

American kamikaze years before Japanese kamikazes existed.

Remember Pearl Harbor (1942) shows all the signs of a worried and confused country that fears all its enemies have been working together. (Nazi spies really had zero to do with Pearl Harbor.) The American characters start off guileless and carefree, living in the happy fantasy that ended for real-life Americans when they went to bed on the night of December 6. The characters pass from cluelessness to helplessness and eventually arrive at the grim realization that the only way to win will be to sacrifice everything. This is a document from a nation reeling from the abrupt transition from peace to war and steeling itself to what it might have to face in the near future.

The following month, Columbia Pictures released *Submarine Raider*, which best exemplifies the anxiety-dream atmosphere of Pearl Harbor movies at this time. Essentially, what happens is that people on a private yacht observe a Japanese submarine in the Pacific Ocean. With this, they become the first Americans to know that Pearl Harbor is to be attacked. The Japanese bomb the yacht and sink it, and there's only one survivor, who is rescued by an American submarine. But all attempts to warn Pearl Harbor fail, and the next thing they know, they're hearing about the attack over the radio. Again and again, this scenario repeats in these Pearl Harbor films: There's crucial, life-saving knowledge, but it can't be transmitted, and yet the characters try and try, until the frenzy climaxes with the inevitable, unstoppable, and unchangeable awfulness being broadcast on the radio.

Perhaps, then, it can be considered a good sign that in September of 1942, 20th Century-Fox released a film that actually *begins* with word of the Pearl Harbor attack. People were getting used to the idea now. They were processing it. The film was *Careful, Soft Shoulder*, and it was a breezy drama about a New York socialite (Virginia Bruce) who finds herself navigating a treacherous environment in which there are Axis agents posing as American agents, and real American agents that she suspects might be Axis agents. By September of 1942, audiences may have been ready for a happy ending, because in *Careful* our heroine makes the right choices, which result in the sinking of a Japanese submarine.

Wake Island, released the same month, was in a grimmer vein, but it also indicates a country getting past shock and settling in for a long siege. As in *Careful, Soft Shoulder*, the Pearl Harbor attack comes early in the story. Based on the real-life defense of Wake Island, it depicts a group of fictional characters attempting to hold the American outpost in the face of a Japanese bombardment. The film implies that the Americans fought to the death, but, in fact, sixteen hundred people (most of them civilian contractors) were taken prisoner. In this early part of the war, there were no victories to make movies about, and so Hollywood was left trying to find inspiration in defeat. The film opens with a credit sequence alluding to Custer's Last Stand, among other "dark hours" in American history—a grim citation.

It says something about the mood of the country that, when the battle scenes were filmed on location in Utah, residents had to be alerted by the media that the Japanese planes flying overhead were props and not the real thing. It would take a pretty massive invasion force to make it all the way from the West Coast to Utah, but understandably no one was thinking straight in those days.

IT'S WITH THIS ATMOSPHERE IN MIND that we can gain some understanding of *Little Tokyo, U.S.A.* (1942), by far the most revealing and disturbing of the World War II propaganda films made during this early period. It's set in Los Angeles, where a respected Japanese American businessman (Harold Huber in yellowface) is, in fact, the head of a group of prominent Japanese Americans secretly working to undermine the United States. There is a token good Japanese, who is murdered by the group, but every other Japanese character in the film is powerful, sneaky, and evil, as well as working in concert with a German American loyal to the Nazis. Preston Foster played a police detective who gets close to uncovering the secret society, and so he is framed for murder and hears of the Pearl Harbor attack while in prison. But eventually, he escapes and breaks the organization. In the climactic moment, he punches the Japanese American businessman and says, "That's for Pearl Harbor, you slant-eyed—" He doesn't complete the sentence because, in 1940s movies, whenever someone is about to say a curse word, something or someone always interrupts.

So far, this plot is just another fever dream, just another World War II movie from 1942. But there's more. The movie next shows a succession of newspaper headlines. The first merely says that the detective broke up the Japanese spy ring. But the next says "All Japs to Be Evacuated." Another says "Last Japs Leave L.A. Today!" This is followed by "Santa Anita Race Track Is Evacuation Station for Japs." And the final one says "'Little Tokyo' Deserted Village." Between shots of these headlines, we see various Los Angeles sites, which appear to be from historical footage, of crowds of Japanese and Japanese Americans with suitcases, looking uncertain, with police standing near them. The accompanying music is curiously without moral comment—it suggests neither human calamity nor the triumph of good over evil. It merely sounds as if big things are happening, that events are coming fast and furious. The most curious sight is that of Little Tokyo, which is indeed a ghost town—empty streets and abandoned storefronts. From the context, it would seem that the movie is presenting this to audiences as a good thing.

The curtain speech makes that message explicit. Brenda Joyce, as the heroine, who happens to be a radio personality, speaks to the city, announcing that "in the interest of national safety, all Japanese—whether citizens or not—are being evacuated from strategic military zones on the Pacific Coast. Unfortunately, in time of war, the loyal must suffer inconvenience with the disloyal."

There it is. When otherwise good people start talking about the innocent needing to suffer along with the guilty, you have a nation turning on itself. When such a notion could be said from a movie screen—keeping in mind that movies are made to appeal not to a majority, but to everyone in an audience—it means that filmmakers knew the sentiment would meet with few or no objections.

California had succumbed to war-induced nativist panic. Ultimately, more than 127,000 Japanese residents, most of them citizens of the United States, would be forced out of their homes and into internment camps.

EVEN AS THE PANIC OF THOSE FIRST MONTHS FADED, Pearl Harbor ensured that people of Japanese ancestry would remain the most hated of America's enemies, widely depicted for the rest of the war as unknowable, robotic, and devious. If there's a happy ending to be found in this story, it's that the United States and Hollywood began to recover their moral sense in comparatively short order. Six years after the war, MGM released *Go for Broke!* (1951), about the 442nd Infantry Regiment, the renowned Japanese American army unit that became the most decorated regiment in the American military. The film also starred actual members of that regiment.

In 1955, Spencer Tracy starred in *Bad Day at Black Rock*, a major production that confronts the issue of anti-Japanese racism. Tracy played a one-armed veteran who comes to a California desert town looking for a man named Komoko, and as soon as he announces his intentions, people clam up and become either fearful or hostile. Eventually, it comes out that Komoko's son saved Tracy's life during the war and was killed, and Tracy wants to present the son's medal to Komoko. But Komoko, as it turns out, was killed in the aftermath of Pearl Harbor by a gang of drunks who set fire to his house and shot him. *Bad Day at Black Rock* was a major film—it was nominated for three Academy Awards—and it confirms the transformation in attitude that had taken place over the intervening decade. Another major award-winning film, *The Bridge on the River Kwai* (1957), presented, in the performance of Sessue Hayakawa, a Japanese prison camp commander as a reasonable, reasoning human being.

Once people are no longer terrified, they're able to remember their humanity. Remembering it when one is frightened is the hard part.

In this same era, Pearl Harbor stopped being portrayed as just a terrifying catastrophe and more as a marker in people's personal lives. *From Here to Eternity* (1953) was the story of several characters living in Hawaii before and after the attack on Pearl Harbor. The movie's indelible image is of Deborah Kerr and Burt Lancaster kissing on the beach. During the war, in the movie *Casablanca*, Humphrey Bogart told Ingrid Bergman that "the problems of three little people don't amount to a hill of beans in this crazy world." People didn't want to believe that, but they needed to, in order to find the strength to put one foot in front of the other as they did things they would otherwise rather not be doing. And now here was a wartime movie with a postwar spirit, which concerned itself with nothing but the problems of little people. America was back to normal.

It would be another generation before Pearl Harbor could be presented as a historical event, with the personal implications obscured and the history highlighted. *Tora! Tora! Tora!* (1970) gave us the war from both sides. Then a generation after that came *Pearl Harbor* (2001), which was little more than a love triangle set against a historical backdrop.

ONE COULD SAY THAT THE PORTRAYAL of Japanese people following the end of World War II rather quickly went back to normal, but, for a community that had experienced racism before the war, normal was never all that good. In 1961, it was still possible, in *Breakfast at Tiffany's*, for Mickey Rooney to play

Holly Golightly's Japanese landlord as a squinting, buck-toothed hysteric, more offensive and demeaning than just about anything you could find in a film from thirty years earlier. However, the portrayal, offensive as it was, may have done some good, albeit unintended, in that its very extremeness created notice even at the time, and now it seems like the end of something that should have ended sooner. The portrayal does, however, mar an otherwise lovely film, and while I would never tamper with a classic or favor the editing of movies to comply with later cultural norms and attitudes, this is one case that might tempt me.

As California has grown over the past hundred years, so has Hollywood and so has America. Visions of orange groves have given way to a complex image of California within the public imagination as something modern, sometimes threatening, sometimes promising, but still embodying aspirations and dreams of the future. That more people are included in that vision and in that dream of the future is a sign of progress, and of a California culture and a movie culture pushing each other forward.

CHAPTER SEVEN

Romance

Certain places are just better than others at communicating romance. If you're in Europe, it's Paris, it's Rome, it's Venice— sometimes, it's even Vienna. In the United States, there's really nothing besides New York City and California, and with New York City, we're really only talking about the island of Manhattan. With California, it's the whole state, not just the big cities but the wild expanses of nature contained in between.

In a California romance, the environment becomes part of the story. A romance set in Cleveland is a set of events that happen to be taking place in a certain location, but the same love affair could be set somewhere else. But California is a collaborator in any romance. These movies tell us that if you're going to fall in love, you might as well do it in California. The beauty of the state adds to and reflects a sense of exhilaration.

Yet, as is always the case with this complicated place, it's not all light. Like love, like lust, California offers the opportunity to get lost. This seems only natural, that the cliffs and the edges, where the wild rocks meet the consuming sea, should be places to lose oneself to passion. California is, after all, the location that people travel to for transformation and heightened experience.

Thus we get the equal and opposite reaction to the surreal paradise of eternal sunshine. This is the dark side, and it has its expression, or at least its analogue, in the natural disasters that have a way of disturbing the tranquility. But mostly the darkness is internal. California dreaming isn't pagan. Often, it's Puritans in a hot tub trying to escape their past and their backgrounds, but not escaping their own inner judgment.

Bob & Carol & Ted & Alice, Paul Mazursky's 1969 film, is a more unsettling than funny comedy of manners about glamorous upper-class, youngish-middle-aged married people whose lives become untethered from anything resembling conventional sexual morality. In its day, the film was praised for its cutting dissection of modern mores, which means that it became dated almost immediately and remains something of a cultural relic. But its insights into the interplay between the ethos embodied by California and the characters' inner sense of what is right are as apt today as ever.

The film's classic ending places all four of the protagonists in the same bed—two married couples about to have an orgy. But suddenly, no one can make the first move. They're glum and embarrassed. They wish they were somewhere else. The question is whether they've been indoctrinated by a morality that they'd do well to shake off but can't, or whether there is a natural understanding of right and wrong that can't be dislodged by fashion.

Either way, the prospect of a joyless orgy doesn't seem difficult to pass up—it hardly seems like the prize at the end of the rainbow of self-realization and years of analysis. It seems a bit tawdry, and even more silly.

In the early 1960s, the Italian director Michelangelo Antonioni said that "Eros is sick" in modern times, and California, as the part of the United States in the advance guard of social thought, became the location of choice for depicting the sicknesses of sex and love in modern American life. This has been the case for at least half a century. A good example of this is *Shampoo* (1975), written by Robert Towne and Warren Beatty and directed by Hal Ashby. It tends to be remembered as the story of a handsome and fortunate hairstylist living an enviable existence—a conflation of our conception of Warren Beatty in that period and the role that he played in the film. In fact, the movie tells a sophisticated story about the distortions and strains that modern life puts on healthy human emotion.

Beatty's hairstylist has a simple and understandable ambition. He wants to start his own salon. He has a possible investor, a rich businessman played by Jack Warden, but there's a complication in that he's having sex with the man's wife (Lee Grant). The hairstylist has two other women in his life, his current girlfriend (Goldie Hawn), and an ex-girlfriend that he really loves (Julie Christie). To further complicate things, this ex-girlfriend is in a relationship with the wealthy businessman.

Throughout, women throw themselves at Beatty, including a very young Carrie Fisher, and the hairstylist has a famous monologue at the end in which he admits everything. ("I fucked 'em all. . . . That's why I went to beauty school.") But far from glamorous, the hairstylist just seems lost and pathetic. He lacks the one currency that could actually give him command of his own life—that is, actual, legal tender currency—and he is otherwise a reed blowing in the wind, at the mercy of his own libido, but also of any caprice or impulse on the part of his rich clients. He is in Beverly Hills, where being handsome and desired merits only an invitation to the party. But the party is in service of the wealthy. Even the rich women who seem obsessed with him are just playing a drama for their own amusement, and they're insulated against consequences in a way that he's not.

What's ultimately at stake for this man? It's not only the prospect of financial autonomy in the form of a hair salon. It's himself, his selfhood. In the final scene, he stands on a hill looking down at Julie Christie, who is going off with Jack Warden. Beatty plays a man of normal natural impulses, with decent sums of empathy and human feeling, and yet his own instincts have led him to an absolute dead end, where he has nothing. His fate seems partly his fault, but partly to do with the world that he inhabits. There's something wrong with this beautiful place, or at least something wrong with what it brings out in people.

No, California isn't safe, even for the man who appears to have everything. It just *seems* safe, which makes it more dangerous. It inspires dreams not of survival but of ultimate fulfillment, and these dreams put people in collision with others pursuing those same dreams, with the same conviction and sense of destiny, or with those who, having achieved their dream, are not going to share. The desolate places of the Earth create a desperation for the basics of existence. Paradise creates an internal drive for ecstasy—for happiness that matches the surroundings.

Take the case of Clint Eastwood in *Play Misty for Me* (1971). He's a deejay, living the classic man-dream, West Coast style. He has a glam beach shack, all crashing waves and jazz tunes on the stereo. He is free from the chains of routine domestic life and the downward suck of all attachments. Carnality enhances this vision, the reward and entitlement of the cool guy. Women come to his side like birds to a feeder. There is no future that could disrupt this dream of freedom, no larger social machinery to shred it. His only problem is that he encounters a woman—a fan (Jessica Walter) who contrives to meet him in a nightclub—who sees him as the fulfillment of her *own* dream. They have sex, and she becomes emotionally attached and soon starts exhibiting unstable and violent behavior. She becomes a threat to his life, to his career, and to those close to him, until he ultimately kills her in self-defense.

The capacity of the sexually ferocious woman to upset a man's perfectly balanced life is not just a feature of 1970s movies. The femme fatale flourished in nineteenth- and early twentieth-century art and literature, and she showed up in the vamp films of the 1910s and twenties. We even find her, albeit in sanitized form, in the films made under the censorship of the Production Code—films such as *Mildred Pierce* (1945) and *The Postman Always Rings Twice* (1946). It's fabulously executed in the portrait of Mildred's daughter, Veda (Ann Blyth), who hates her mother and uses her as a stepping-stone to a lover and money. She is a bad seed, but also a product of her time and place. Likewise, Cora (Lana Turner) in *Postman* marinates in a combination of lust and greed, while living a boring existence in a California truck stop, perched somewhere in the valley between no place and nowhere.

The femme fatale is a product of misogyny and sexual

terror, and she usually finds a foothold in eras in which sex is associated with danger. But Jessica Walter in *Misty* is outside the usual femme fatale pattern, in that the peace she disrupts with her sexuality is the hero's peace of ongoing sex with *other* women. Perhaps this is just a more modern formulation of an older archetype. In any case, our hero does have an ex-girlfriend (Donna Mills), and he and she get back together, and so the evil woman goes after the girlfriend. Still, it seems that what she's really disrupting is the happiness and freedom of being a man-about-town in Carmel-by-the-Sea, California.

By the time we get to Robert Altman's *Short Cuts* in 1993, women are no longer the sole repositories of rapacious sexual impulse, but Eros still is not well. The Altman film, which artfully combines a number of Raymond Carver stories into one ensemble narrative, is like an amalgam of various emotional and sexual distortions, which have become, for one prototypical group of Los Angeles inhabitants, so familiar as to have become normalized. In one segment, men go off on a fishing trip and find the corpse of a young woman washed up on the shore. Instead of retracing their steps and reporting the discovery to the authorities, they tie the body to some rocks and proceed to enjoy a rare weekend away.

Meanwhile, Jennifer Jason Leigh plays a wife and mother who earns extra money by working for a sex chat line. It's meant to be comical. We see her performing domestic chores while lethargically engaging in sex talk, but there's something unsettling about this all the same, the sense of domesticity and sex both losing their force and meaning.

It's appropriate that a movie that concerns itself with the

distortions that environment places on love should end with the worst possible violation, and that the environment itself should become involved. While walking in a barren, rocky area, a man (Chris Penn) tries to rape a woman and then, in a burst of rage, he kills her by hitting her over the head with a rock. But just at that moment, there's an earthquake and a rockslide, which means that his crime will be attributed to the natural disaster. Here's a case where the message is almost too explicit, in that the earthquake doesn't seem like a coincidence but like a product of the same inherent perversity that also caused the murder; the perversity is intrinsic to the place.

IT COULD BE ARGUED THAT THE SPIRITUAL SICKNESS we see in these films is caused by money's damaging influence. But the truth may be slightly different, that spiritual sickness is rather a luxury *afforded* by money. When people have the freedom that money makes available, it's then possible for them to live unfettered lives and get themselves into trouble. Likewise, it becomes possible for a prosperous collective to create a world of confusion for themselves, which they can't escape because they have no baseline available for spiritual health or normality.

Consider *Petulia*, set in San Francisco and released in that disturbed year of 1968. At one point, someone introduces "Bobby Kennedy" as a conversational topic. Meanwhile, Kennedy died four days before the film was released. Such was the ever-changing horror show of America that the film was made in and released into.

The title character, played by Julie Christie, is a married

British woman who tries to pick up a doctor (George C. Scott) at a charity ball at the Fairmont Hotel. She is zany and impulsive and seems, for about thirty seconds, to be the kind of free-spirited character that Goldie Hawn might have played in the same era. But no, this is a dark film. Petulia has a disturbed husband (Richard Chamberlain) who beats her. She wants to seduce the doctor, but she doesn't want to. She acts on impulse, but her impulses change from one moment to the next, and the sense we get is of a time and place without stricture or grounding, in which people are finding their own way, and they're unhappy. Meanwhile, pushing at them from the ground up is this unsettled world of young people, with their strange heroes and heroines, such as the Grateful Dead and Janis Joplin, who actually appear in the film.

In *Petulia*, director Richard Lester presents San Francisco as a trendsetting archetype, interesting in its way and glamorous, if observed from a distance. Lester knew something about glamour and about universal loci of cool, having filmed the Beatles movie *A Hard Day's Night* in the London of 1964. But while that earlier film presented a burst of joy, *Petulia* shows a world in which love has been corrupted, perhaps cheapened by casual encounters, so that it no longer has meaning; or perhaps it's that the casualness of sex has detached it from mystery, so that the meaninglessness of it all has been revealed for all to recognize. Either way, there's a pervasive sense of people knowing too much and that all that knowledge, as well as all that wealth, has just uncovered a huge emptiness.

WE SEE NOTHING LIKE THIS SPIRITUAL SICKNESS some forty years later in *Going the Distance* (2010), a courtship drama—one hesitates to call it a romantic comedy—about a young couple trying to hold on to their relationship during the recession. Drew Barrymore and Justin Long meet but, by some miracle, she gets a writing job at the *San Francisco Chronicle*. She has no choice but to take it. Jobs, in general, are scarce during the recession, and newspaper jobs are close to nonexistent. So they must endure the strain of a love sustained by phone calls and by cross-country trips that they can barely afford. Again, there is something about the need to survive that clears away the cobwebs of confusion and neurosis. There is also something about pressure of this kind to help define the primacy of love in a human life, as something bound up with survival, emotional and otherwise.

Two years later, *The Five-Year Engagement* (2012) also dealt with the pressures of jobs and finances on a relationship. In this film, Jason Segel and Emily Blunt live in San Francisco, where he is a sous-chef and she has just earned a doctorate. They're engaged to be married, but they put it off when she gets a position at the University of Michigan in Ann Arbor. He quits his job and follows her, and suddenly San Francisco has never looked so good—not only to the characters, but to the audience watching. Everyone in Michigan is freezing. The light makes everything look old and dingy, not bright in the California light. He finds no equivalent restaurant to work in and begins to fall apart for lack of meaningful employment.

After a lot of ups and downs and trials in the relationship, the film concludes with a wedding service in Alamo Square Park, famous of its view of the "Painted Lady" Victorian houses that are lined up, side by side, across the street. In the post-millennium version of San Francisco, the city is no longer so complacent in its opulence that it is prey to spiritual disease. It's rather the place of arrival, the place where love makes sense.

This presentation of San Francisco has become a familiar, and it's genuinely in keeping with the character of the city. There is something wistful and outside time about San Francisco, something fundamentally benevolent that makes it a supportive environment for movie romance. This is the case even in a film like *Butterflies Are Free* (1972), which was based on a stage play. We see very little of the North Beach neighborhood in which it's set. The movie goes outside only briefly, to show the blind protagonist, played by Edward Albert, going about his routine—a certain number of steps to the store, etc. The scene is to show that he has a degree of autonomy. He can function in his life. But at the same time, just that tiny bit of North Beach is enough to make us feel the circumscription of his existence, that he is effectively barred from seeing the romance of the place he's in. This absence is filled, at least temporarily, in the form of his next-door neighbor, played by Goldie Hawn, who represents—for us and for him—his chance to bring into his apartment the unseen romance of the outside and make it tangible. His immediate, passionate, desperate attachment to this woman after a single sexual encounter is made all the more forceful because we've been outside with him. All the world is there, but there's nothing there for him. His only chance at having anything is for it to enter within those four walls.

Something of this idea of romance and confinement can be found in *Cherish* (2002), a lovely movie from writer-director

Finn Taylor that did less than nothing at the box office but needs to be discovered as one of the best movies of its year. Perhaps the reason for audience indifference is that it communicates a subtle idea and requires its audience be receptive to subtlety. It's about a woman (Robin Tunney) under house arrest for something she didn't do. Meanwhile, she's being stalked by a dangerous maniac.

The soundtrack is suffused by pop songs, most of them songs of yearning, such as "Cherish," by the Association. By placing them in this context, Taylor makes us realize the almost-lunatic subjectivity of these songs and of love songs in general: They speak from a murderously selfish universe in which only the singer's feelings matter. Yet at the same time, the movie depicts a world of deep, sincere longing—the healthy kind—in its presentation of the man whose court-appointed job it is to check on the woman every day and see that her ankle-bracelet tracking device is intact and functioning. We see the woman as she really is, which is how this man sees her. And we see her as the stalker imagines her, in objectified, romanticized terms.

In a sense, this is a film in which everyone is trapped inside his or her own pop song, including the woman, who is also trapped inside her apartment. And the question is, how does anyone escape this trap of ego and need and actually make a connection with another person? For the stalker, who is distorted beyond the possibility of redemption, there is no reality outside the cage of self. For the others, there's an awareness of the outside, just no clear means of getting there.

The San Francisco connection—why this is a San Francisco and not a Detroit story—is contained in the promise of the city itself, even in this version of San Francisco, which is rather dingy and is shown late at night. With San Francisco, the light usually shines through the darkness, which is in keeping with this film's story.

A year later, *Dopamine* (2003) also showed a decidedly unromantic vision of the city, while conveying an earned and grounded romantic universe. Directed and cowritten by Mark Decena, it is an affecting love story about a troubled artist (Sabrina Lloyd) and a software designer (John Livingston). Decena set the action in a version of the city its younger residents would know, not the Painted Ladies San Francisco but a city of neighborhood bars, old lofts, and sterile working spaces, as if to say that beautiful things can grow in these quotidian, pedestrian places.

The man has this idea that all emotions are chemical, as if the fact that they're chemical makes them less real in the experience of them. (The title refers to the feel-good chemical that signals pleasure in the brain.) Meanwhile, the woman is trying to chemically anaesthetize herself from a personal trauma she can't forget. (For the multiple takes it took to film one scene, Lloyd had to smoke so many cigarettes that an oxygen tank had to be brought onto the set so she could breathe.) So it's a romance between one person who denies feeling and another who wants to be numb.

The emotions are very California—not closed off, exactly, and not dignified, as in some of the more reticent parts of the country. Some regions express emotion and some regions repress it, but the California style is different—it's to suppress emotion while presenting a glib front to the world, as though acting as one's own press agent. In *Dopamine*, it takes a while to move past that, but when the protagonists are finally able to let down their guard, we believe that they've fought their way to a bond that's healing and lasting.

Love is a familiar healer and educator in many screen romances. In California romances, the environment becomes part of the healing. *Sweet November* (1968) is a lovely time-capsule romance, set in New York, about a hard-driving, emotionally disconnected man who meets an endearingly quirky woman who adopts him as her special project: Apparently, she takes a new lover at the start of every month, each time choosing a man who needs to be fixed in some way. The 2001 remake, set in San Francisco, starred Keanu Reeves as the man chosen to be Charlize Theron's November project.

The film becomes a meditation on the preciousness of time and the brevity of life and love. At one point, Reeves walks out of the apartment and takes in the world around him. He sees kids playing on a street in the Potrero Hill neighborhood, with the whole San Francisco cityscape behind them, and he is stopped by the beauty of the moment.

One of the best uses of San Francisco in recent years can be found in Barry Jenkins's *Medicine for Melancholy* (2008), about the twenty-four hours following a one-night stand: A man and a woman wake up at a party, following a drunken romp, feeling hung over and embarrassed. But as framed by Jenkins, the world around them looks beautiful and full of promise.

Jenkins films the action in a washed-out color palette that almost looks black-and-white, except that little details will occasionally pop out, such as the color of the sky. Jenkins intends for us to notice the surrounding world as something present yet separate from the characters. Very early in the film, we are able to perceive two realities—life as the characters are experiencing it, and the life that seems right there, available to them, if only *they* would see it.

It's common and often poignant for filmmakers to film romantic characters in a hyper-real and sometimes ugly environment, so that we sense both the cloud of happiness they're in and the world that they're up against. *Medicine for Melancholy* is the rare film that does the opposite—it shows realistic, almost cynical characters against a romantic background that calls out to them. We root for them to hear the call. Though calm and matter-of-fact in its presentation, with nothing overt or insistent about it, the film churns with the filmmaker's wonder and fascination. As in *Dopamine*, the question is whether its two protagonists will overcome their impulse for self-protection and find their way toward connection. As always, San Francisco is there to help.

Los Angeles is less often complicit in bringing people together. Most of the time, it merely colors relationships; it doesn't bring them into being. It presents an ideal that can't be penetrated. It's a place of ache more than fulfillment, a beautiful dream and a sterile reality. In *Poetic Justice* (1993), Tupac Shakur and Janet Jackson meet and fall in love. But although they meet in Los Angeles, it takes a road trip to the central coast for them to discover their mutual affection. They stop on the side of the road and sit together, looking down at the crashing water and the timeless rock formations.

Steve Martin made one of the strongest cases for Los Angeles as a place for love and romance with *L.A. Story* (1991), a celebration that's both sincere and tongue-in-cheek. It shows the pretension of Los Angeles, the sometimes amusing strangeness of it and the faddism of it, but from the indulgent view that it's all indicative of something deeper and more admirable—a genuine willingness of the heart. Through the story of a weatherman (Martin) who falls in love with a British journalist (Victoria Tennant), Martin, who wrote the screenplay, tells us that however easy they are to mock, the excesses of Los Angeles are just as easy to forgive, once you realize that they're all caused by a questing of the spirit—by people trying to find ideal ways to live. As the British journalist in the film observes, Los Angeles is a place where "they've taken a desert and turned it into their dreams."

IN MOVIES, CALIFORNIA PUTS PEOPLE into contact with nature, and their own nature blooms. They become what they were always meant to be. This is most vividly expressed in Alfonso Arau's *A Walk in the Clouds*, a 1995 romance set in the Napa Valley wine region. A returning World War II veteran (Keanu Reeves) meets an unmarried pregnant woman (Aitana Sánchez-Gijón) from a wealthy Mexican winemaking family, and he agrees to pose as her husband for one day. But nature has its way. In Arau's vision, Napa is a land of amber sunsets and misty dawns. When the characters walk along the vines in the morning, the mist makes them look as though they're walking on clouds. Later, Sánchez-Gijón crushes grapes in a high-spirited dance that's elemental, signaling the union of nature, lust, and love—and the beginning of the lovers' becoming the fully realized people they were meant to be.

This process of becoming is never entirely romantic or easy. In fact, the journey, as we see in the better California films, is demanding. It inspires as much doubt as it does certainty and often occasions hard choices.

The Sandpiper (1965) is one of those older California movies that is ready to be seen again. Movies, like everything else, start out new. And then, particularly if they were topical or innovative, they enter an awkward middle age after about twenty years, during which everything about them seems passé. Often this is especially the case with movies that were influential, because, over time, we become so familiar with the movies they influenced that the original source seems like a collection of clichés. Only time can sort this out, as the lesser movies, inspired by the original, fade from memory, and the issues, techniques, and styles of another time feel less out of date and more classic. Not every movie recovers from middle age. Most die there. But the best movies make it through, and in that category, ready again for its close-up, we find *The Sandpiper*, starring Elizabeth Taylor and Richard Burton.

Just those two names have made the movie hard to assess for decades. In the mid-1960s, Taylor and Burton were *the* glamour couple of the world. And then, ten years later, they were older, and he was a struggling alcoholic, and she was struggling with her weight, so that they seemed more like tabloid fodder than artists—especially so when they were together. But now it has been more than fifty years, time enough to recognize that the then-married pair made one bona fide classic, *Who's Afraid of Virginia Woolf?* (1966), and this one near-classic a year earlier, a quintessential and astute California romance.

It's a surprising thing that classics are so often topical, dealing with the concerns and the events of their very specific place in time. Why should films such as these have a timeless resonance? Partly it's because an era is at its least self-conscious when it's responding to something that has just happened or is happening, when the era is in conversation with itself. Sometimes saying something simple results in statements that are pure and direct and that connect with the future as well as the present.

Thus, we get a story that sounds so sixties: Taylor is a free-spirited artist, living in a beach house on Big Sur, in touch with elemental nature, either an atheist or a pagan, but either way unconventional, and Burton plays the headmaster of an Episcopal boarding school, which the artist's son is forced to attend after repeatedly getting into trouble. This throws into contact these two very attractive people, who happen to have completely opposite beliefs and philosophies. He is a married man whose head-bound life of responsibility has become all too routine, and she is a turbulent woman who is absolutely sure of everything, including when she's not exactly right. Even if they didn't look like Elizabeth Taylor and Richard Burton, you could see how these people might be attractive to each other.

The idea that a free spirit can help unlock an uptight gentleman is such a cliché of the 1960s that another movie like that would be hardly worth watching. Yet *The Sandpiper* is not pushing a cultural agenda, but rather making an observation about human need. The woman lives in constant communion with the sea and sky, and this informs her understanding of life. He is the man from civilization, with all that implies, both bad and good. In a lesser movie, she'd be the spontaneous paragon that he learns to live up to. In *The Sandpiper*, the two have a lot to teach other.

She upends his life. He winds up quitting his job, taking time off to travel, and separating from his very nice wife of many years as he goes off to find himself. Meanwhile, Elizabeth Taylor's character agrees to leave her son in the Episcopal school, recognizing that the routine and environment are good for him. Both lovers know, without even having to say it, that they are too different, in faith and temperament, to be together. But in a tough way, they've done each other good, and each has found a more complete way of seeing things.

In a sense, *The Sandpiper*—though very much of its time, and very much a vehicle for two major stars—occupies an ideal space between the dark and light of California romance, presenting nature as a genuine and worthwhile force in human life and relationships, while acknowledging that natural impulse is not infallible, that people need the rational as well as the visceral.

What's imperative, the movie seems to imply, is that the intuitive and feeling side of life should not be lost, because the whole push and strain of life tends toward denying it. That is why California artists who live on the beach are very important, even when the art they create is only so-so.

CHAPTER EIGHT
Heinous Crime

At the start of Alfred Hitchcock's *Psycho* (1960), Janet Leigh steals $40,000 because she needs the money. She and her lover are in a hotel room talking about how they wish they could be together all the time, but they can't, because he's in debt. So later that afternoon, when she's entrusted by her employer to make a bank deposit of $40,000 in cash, temptation overwhelms her and she takes off down the road.

This is the kind of crime that anyone can understand. Most of us might even sympathize. In fact, we *know* we sympathize when we see that a highway patrolman is following her and we want her to get away. Her crime is immoral, and if everyone behaved that way, commerce and organized society would be impossible to sustain. Nonetheless, we get it. *She really needs the money.* She's stealing from an extremely rich guy who won't even feel the loss. And she's not getting any younger. She wants to have a life. Her crime makes sense to us.

It should be noted that when Leigh's character, Marion Crane, commits this sensible, understandable crime, she is in

Phoenix, Arizona, and that when she skips town, she heads west. That's her second mistake, and an even worse one than stealing the $40,000.

Indeed, it would fit right in with the era and with the movie if, at the moment of crossing the California border, the camera were to swerve to show Rod Serling in a black suit, standing next to a cactus. Marion has entered a Twilight Zone. She has left a world where crime makes sense and entered a strange state where it doesn't—where often the whole *point* of crime is that it doesn't.

This is the realm of perversity. In movies set in other states, people usually commit crimes to advance their own self-interest. In California movies, that motive, if it exists at all, is secondary. The primary motive—sometimes unconscious, but often very conscious—is to communicate despair or rage or rejection, or to instill panic, or to convey a sense of nihilism and absurdity. It's to create suspicion, both in the victims and the general public, that life is not what we thought it was.

Or, to put it another way, in movies set in other places, criminals do things, even though they know it's wrong, either because they don't care about right and wrong or because they'd rather be wrong than do without. But in California movies, they engage in crime *because* it's wrong, because, on some level, they want other people to feel sick about it.

As such, there is an extra dimension to the crime movies set in California, one that might be called metaphysical or existential. They're statements about life. The criminals are saying, "Real life is not your life. It's this horrible thing that *I* think it is." This impulse needn't be conscious. The motive of Norman Bates

(Anthony Perkins) when he kills Ms. Crane in the shower isn't to prove something. He doesn't know why he's doing it or even *that* he's doing it. He's out of his mind. Even so, he's communicating his hell, moving it out of his head and presenting it, lethal and intact, to this other, random person. He stands nothing to gain. He's a purely perverse entity.

This California notion of crime as the ultimate expression not of self-interest but of perversity makes it inevitable that film noir, when it emerged, should be based almost entirely in California. We'll look at noir in a separate chapter as a specifically California product, as something that could not have originated anywhere else. That's a subject unto itself, with a large history. This chapter will confine itself, in general terms, to crime as presented in movies set in California and to what those films have to say.

One of the insidious things about crime in California, which the movies capture, is that it often has a way of sneaking up on people. If you watch a crime film set in New York, you expect something awful will come leaping out from the shadows. Even non-crime films set in New York can make you think of crime. When Samantha (Kim Cattrall) walks around the meatpacking district in the *Sex and the City* movie (2008), we tend to look to the edges of the frame to make sure everything is okay. And because it's a comedy, it always is.

However, to anyone outside California, the gang-ridden South Central Los Angeles neighborhood presented in *Boyz n the Hood* (1991) looks pleasantly residential. People live in houses, not in awful apartment buildings with scary elevators and stairways. These California houses may be dingy and in need of repair, but they're painted in pastel colors. This is not the Wu-Tang Clan rapping from the Park Hill projects on Staten Island. South Central is a rough place that, to the uninformed eye, doesn't look rough at all.

Boyz n the Hood, John Singleton's masterpiece, is the story of young, sensible people growing up in the midst of madness and trying to find ways to survive within it. In an extended prologue, a ten-year-old boy is walking home from school and sees blood on the sidewalk. A little girl asks him why the blood is yellow, and he answers, "That's what happens when it separates from the plasma." This is what he already knows at ten years old.

The film's soundscape is unique, with helicopters and planes passing overhead, as if to emphasize how trapped the people are down below. But Singleton knew something about violent places: Even war zones are not violent every minute of the day, and so he lets scenes breathe. There are long conversations. There's a sense of languor that persuades us to relax as the characters themselves almost relax, so that each time violence erupts, we experience the appropriate shock.

At the same time, the filmmaker forces us to understand that the characters' experience is not necessarily the same as the audience's. There's a scene in which two teenagers, just walking home having a conversation, realize that a car full of guys with shotguns and machine guns are driving around with the intention of killing them. They don't react with incredulity or outrage. They react as though they have a very big, practical problem that must be solved.

Cuba Gooding, Jr., and Morris Chestnut played the two boys trying to escape South Central. Ice Cube is unforgettable as a young gang member who knows he is on a road to nowhere and that he cannot get off. He is an intelligent, thinking person who feels he must act out his part in a mad world, even though he knows that this means he'll be dead in a matter of days. Like Burt Lancaster in the classic noir *The Killers* (1946), he won't run, just wait.

What places *Boyz n the Hood* within the long tradition of California crime films is the sense that the violence we're seeing is violence for no reason. It is something that is growing out of a condition, to be sure, but the specific precipitators of the murders are like pretexts, as if the participants were on a treadmill that never stops.

Boyz n the Hood predated the Los Angeles riots by a year. The riots, as well as their catalytic event—the acquittal of the police officers who'd participated in the Rodney King beating—put the focus on Los Angeles as a place of chaos. Thus, we get *Menace II Society* (1993), by the Hughes Brothers, a film that's yet darker and bleaker than *Boyz n the Hood*, bespeaking a world in which virtually all the connections to sedate normality have been severed.

Menace II Society begins with an incident in a Korean grocery store. The owner insults one of the young black men, O-Dog (Larenz Tate), and he responds by killing the owner and his wife, stealing their money, and taking the surveillance tape out of the VHS player. You would think that this last move would be just a matter of self-preservation, of getting rid of the evidence. But no, this is a California crime, and so it's a souvenir. O-Dog *likes* the tape. He plays it for everybody.

The focus of the movie is Caine (Tyrin Turner), who was with O-Dog when he committed the murders, and so Caine is also legally implicated in the crime. For much of the movie, Caine tries to moderate O-Dog, to calm him down and have him stop taking dangerous risks. But Caine is living in a crazy world in which even a reasonable personality could easily end up killing somebody. He has a loving grandmother and aspirations beyond this place, but he still goes around carrying a gun, which he uses to hijack cars, and he sells crack.

There's no higher force in his world, and certainly no authority figure, that represents any higher value. The police are just as twisted as the criminals. At one point, they pull over Caine and a friend and beat them for no reason. Just as the world these characters live in makes no sense, the movie refuses to follow an expected pattern. O-Dog survives the film, while Caine is killed in a drive-by shooting.

This idea that a rough environment compromises everyone is touched on, albeit more gently, in Rick Famuyiwa's brilliant *Dope* (2015), a movie that maintains a comic atmosphere even as we're made to worry, from start to finish, that the protagonist may be killed. A kind of *Risky Business* set in the Los Angeles hood, it stars Shameik Moore as Malcolm, a straight-A student with aspirations to get into Harvard. But first he has to survive living in Inglewood, where every day, on the way home from school, he has a choice—either to ride his bike past a loitering group of drug dealers or to go the other way, past an equally menacing pack of gang members.

Malcolm, who is into 1990s hip hop (perhaps the movie's tribute to the urban crime films of that decade), finds himself in a no-win situation when a drug dealer, facing arrest, stashes heroin, a gun, and an iPhone in Malcolm's backpack. What can he do?

Competing factions want the drugs, so he's in trouble no matter whom he gives the bag to. And he knows that, as a black teenager, going to the police with a bag full of drugs and a gun is not really an option—especially not if he still hopes to go to Harvard. A prison stint wouldn't look good on his college application.

The movie is the story of how Malcolm threads his way to the outcome that he wants, reacting and improvising all the time. The significant turn here is that the Harvard businessman that he is supposed to impress is, in fact, a drug kingpin, and the way he guarantees admittance into Harvard is by threatening the businessman with exposure if Malcolm does not get in. So once again, the idea is reinforced that the world within the hood is just a more violent reflection of the world outside, and that our young hero's task, whether in it or out of it, is the same: To navigate the perfidy of others on his way to a fixed goal. Here, as in film noir, the world is rigged, and there's no safe space.

THE OVERARCHING IDEA HERE is that life makes no sense and the crimes are just special illustrations of that reality. In these tales from the hood, made by African American filmmakers, nothing can make sense because nothing is allowed to make sense, because the environment, which precedes the birth of these characters, won't permit it. But in other California movies an equally familiar pattern—indeed, the more familiar pattern—is for acts of perversity to erupt not as a response to externals but to something internal within the psyche or the life of the era. The crime becomes an expression of some repressed sickness within the culture at large.

Dirty Harry (1971) is most remembered today for the first scene, which introduced audiences to the first of Clint Eastwood's memorable movie catchphrases, "Do I feel lucky?" What's less remembered is that the film is basically a fictionalized retelling of the Zodiac killings, which had begun in the San Francisco Bay Area just two years before and remained (and still remains) unsolved. As in the real-life killings, the murderer keeps communicating with San Francisco media, insisting on coverage and threatening to kill again.

The movie suggests, not only through the character of the serial killer but that of the rogue cop, a society that's unraveling, in which a trigger-happy, borderline crazy policeman is the person best suited for survival. The streets have become war zones, with firefights in the middle of the day, and rural excursions by people just wanting to get away end in death, because there's no escape. The appeal of *Dirty Harry* is in the audience's vicarious connection with Harry's power, as it tapped into audience anxiety that everything was going to hell.

Dirty Harry can be seen as the father of several crime films that followed. *Death Wish* (1974) tells the story of a mild-mannered citizen who becomes a vigilante after his wife is murdered and his daughter is raped by intruders. But being a New York and not a California story, it was different. It was, in structure, a rags-to-riches story, in which a lowly person rises to importance and self-realization through courageous action. And though the world in which the hero existed was chaotic and bestial, *Death Wish* posited that a single man could make a difference. In *Death Wish*, the actions of the vigilante, played by Charles Bronson, cause the crime rate to plummet, and the ending—a fairly happy ending—shows our hero relocating to Chicago, where it's strongly implied that he'll resume his vigilante activities. This is in contrast to *Dirty Harry*, which ends with the hero throwing in the towel. In the New York answer to the California story, one sad, lonely, grief-stricken pacifist can find happiness and purpose and solve an entire city's problems by picking up a gun. But not in California, where no one can in any way do anything good at all.

Dirty Harry is a kind of antecedent, as well, to *Training Day* (2001), which goes a step further to make the rogue cop not an antihero but a villain. It complicates audience expectation by having that villain played by Denzel Washington, employing all the force of his movie-star charm and charisma, for a story in which he's pretty much setting up his new partner (Ethan Hawke) to take the fall for crimes that he himself committed. It's another portrait of urban madness in which everyone is, to some degree, corrupt. The dirty cop's only practical problem is that he has made himself conspicuous by pushing the corruption beyond normal limits.

Zodiac (2007) attempted to tell, in earnest, the story that *Dirty Harry* fictionalized, that of the Zodiac Killer. Director David Fincher earnestly recreated the look of San Francisco in the 1960s and shot footage on location at the *San Francisco Chronicle* to tell the story of reporters working the case. Fincher gives us shots of local landmarks, such as Original Joe's restaurant, and he seems to know exactly what stage of construction the Transamerica Pyramid was in at the time, and he remembers, as few filmmakers do, that during this period and through the 1980s, the Embarcadero Freeway obstructed views of the Ferry

Building at the end of Market Street. Fincher is also one of the few filmmakers working in color to remember that San Francisco is hardly an example of sunny California. The city is gray and cloudy most of the time, and he uses and emphasizes that look to create a murky atmosphere, which is in keeping with the story.

Ultimately, *Zodiac* has the dramatic disadvantages of all true stories that end without resolution. Since it intends to convey a true history that is still without closure, the movie can't offer a dramatically satisfying conclusion. Fincher tries to make up for that by making the atmosphere as murky as the case. In a way, there's no better means of conveying the idea of senselessness than by presenting a case that never makes sense, that never gets solved. The questions stay suspended like the dust illuminated by the fluorescent lights under which the reporters and cops struggle and worry and must come to terms with their own futility.

THE TRUTH IS THAT CALIFORNIA FILMMAKERS needn't make up heinous crime stories. They can just take them from the headlines—or from history. *The Changeling* (2008), an excellent film from Clint Eastwood, touches on a series of real-life murders of boys and young men in the 1920s and '30s. And the murders by the Manson family have sprouted a cottage industry of true-crime films, as well as a recent fictionalized rendering in Quentin Tarantino's *Once Upon a Time . . . in Hollywood* (2019).

Tarantino best relates the phenomenon of serial killing—and the Manson killing in particular—to California and to the ethos surrounding Hollywood. One of the ways he does this is with a pair of parallel shots. In the first, Sharon Tate (Margot Robbie) goes to a theater to see her latest movie. In a state of quiet rapture at this promising period of her life, and thrilled to be part of this thing called the movies, she puts her feet up on the seat in front of her and watches herself in the movie. Interestingly, the "self" that we see on screen is not Robbie but the real Sharon Tate. Tarantino is not trying to fool us. He's purposely showing us the real woman as a way of stepping out of the movie's reality to remind us of what ultimately happened to her.

No more than a half hour of screen time later, we get the parallel shot. Margaret Qualley plays a member of the Manson family who is hitchhiking on a busy Los Angeles street. Brad Pitt, playing a Hollywood stuntman, picks her up, and as he drives, she puts her bare feet up on the dashboard—and hers are dirty from walking the streets. So there they are—two women, roughly the same age. They've come to a place of dreams. They've come to a place to realize their fantasies of themselves. One winds up elevated, ascended into a cloud of self-realization and wealth . . . and the other ends up with her fantasies and grandiosity fueling evil and madness. One's barefoot journey into the California desert guides her to an oasis, where she walks on rose petals; the other winds up with sand, concrete, and the imminence of violence.

The endpoints are different, but the starting points are the same—both have taken a chance in the direction of dreams.

Matthew Bright's *Freeway*, an independent film from 1996, offers an interesting inflection on the usual California serial killer genre. It presents a teenage girl from the most horrific of possible backgrounds: Her mother is a prostitute. Her father is gone. Her stepfather is a pimp and keeps trying to have sex with her. And when she runs off on her own, to avoid being placed in foster care, she gets picked up by a seemingly nice, respectable school counselor (Kiefer Sutherland), who turns out to be a serial killer. One of his fixations is having sex with teenage girls . . . after they're dead.

What makes the film a comedy (believe it or not) is that the movie invests its teenage protagonist with a completely unaccountable sense of self-worth and a skewed but definite moral center. "Why are you killing all them girls, Bob?" she asks accusingly, a line that invariably gets a laugh from the audience because of its bluntness and purity. Why, indeed. The fact that there isn't and cannot be an answer to that question places *Freeway* very much in the California tradition. But the fact that it features a heroine who has not only a sense of right and wrong but also an ability to stand outside the madness and react with more anger than despair or cynicism makes it a California story with a difference.

Most of the time, it's almost as if people in California crime movies expect the bad and only react when things become beyond-belief heinous, as in *The Black Dahlia* (2006), Brian De Palma's screen treatment of the James Ellroy novel based on a horrible 1940s murder in which a woman was dismembered. Likewise, in *Chinatown* (1974), set in the 1930s, it's not enough that people are killing each other over water rights and the diversion of water from Northern to Southern California. That would seem to be enough for a dramatic story, or at least one set in another location, but this is the Golden State, and so there must also be an element of sickness, which in this case is a father

(John Huston) who has fathered a child with his own daughter (Faye Dunaway). When it all blows up and people are dead, what is there to say besides, "Forget it . . . it's Chinatown." This is the place where heinous things happen.

Always, there's the extra dose of senselessness, or of cruelty, or of strange bad fortune.

THOUGH WE DON'T NORMALLY THINK OF THEM as crime films, both versions of *Invasion of the Body Snatchers* (1956 and the 1978 remake) depict the worst kind of crime imaginable—the wholesale theft of body and soul, accomplished on a global scale, done for the purpose of stealing an entire planet. This is the grandest of grand larcenies combined with the most massive of mass murders.

As a concept, *Invasion of the Body Snatchers* has remained in common currency since the original film gradually seeped into the consciousness of the general public. (It was a low-budget production, and it took a while.) Ever since, the notion of "pod people" has, like "drinking the Kool-Aid," become a catchphrase metaphor for any kind of phenomenon that turns people into zombies of conformity.

In its first incarnation, *Invasion* was thought of as an allegory either for McCarthyism or for the encroaching communist threat. Such is the flexibility of the allegory that it can be used in the service of opposing political viewpoints. In terms of McCarthyism, the film works as a story of enforced conformity; as a metaphor about communism, it shows what a society is like when all differences in thought and behavior have been rendered unlawful and when people stamp out their own individuality. It shows what it might be like to have a functioning soul in the midst of totalitarianism.

Yet *Invasion of the Body Snatchers* would not have lasted past the Cold War if it were merely an allegory, nor would it have lasted to this day if it were just a sci-fi concept picture. Rather, there is something in the story that speaks to the deep fears of everyone within the society—the clash between the need to belong and the need to remain true to oneself; the terror of being alone and the equal terror of belonging too much, of being subsumed by the group.

That danger of subsumption is all too real and grounded in human flaw—the one that means people often feel at their most powerful when they are most enslaved. A Hitler Youth standing in a throng with ten thousand other Hitler Youths at a Nuremberg rally, hailing Hitler, identifies with the collective power of the mass and sees himself as an expression of some bold, unstoppable movement. No one ever imagines himself as a cog in a machine, most especially when functioning precisely as a cog in a machine. The machine maker always gives you something else to look at besides the chains on your ankles and the backs of the other galley slaves.

In both versions of *Invasion*—the first takes place in the fictional small town of Santa Mira, and the second in San Francisco—people can be taken over (and replaced by an emotionless blank replica of themselves) only when sleeping. So everyone has to stay awake, even though it's impossible to stay awake all the time. Impossible, yet necessary. In a sense, this is the challenge of living some kind of awakened life, to be vigilant in the face of anything that wants to take over your mind, deaden your emotions, and curtail your capacity for independent thought. Don Siegel, who directed the original, said that he knew "pod people" in the movie industry. *Invasion of the Body Snatchers* crystallizes, in story form, a spiritual threat that all people face.

But what, you might ask, is the California angle in all of this, aside from the fact that the film takes place in California? The short answer, obviously, is to ask how could such a tale originate anywhere *besides* California? The depth of the crime alone, the twistedness, the weirdness of it, the unthinkable horror of it— all that makes this just the kind of thing that would happen in California and nowhere else.

But it's also appropriately a California story because the place itself embodies the main issues explored in the film: the terror of conformity and the obligation to conform. It's a place where everyone wants to be an amazing individual, but not for the sake of individual expression so much as for the approval of the group. In this way, there is always a tension.

Indeed, it's appropriate that, for the remake, director Philip Kaufman moved the action from the nondescript fictional American Santa Mira to the more concrete and specific San Francisco. Here is a city where no one wants to conform, and yet everyone wants to be praised as a nonconformist, and where the easiest way to be called "very brave" is to express an opinion that absolutely no one can disagree with. When people leave their hometowns and travel to the edge of the continent to be with people who are just like themselves, they tend to get annoyed by people who are not like themselves.

Of all places, then, to be infected by a disease that is secretly sought. If everyone is a pod person, at least there will be no more arguments at Thanksgiving dinner. There will be no more clashing thoughts, because there'll be no more thoughts, at all. It's an enforced peace.

By the way, there have since been two other remakes—one, titled *Body Snatchers*, is a low-budget, not-scary 1993 version set on a military base, and the other, *The Invasion*, stars Nicole Kidman and is set in Washington, D.C.

Predictably, only the two California versions end in horror. In 1956, the hero is vainly trying to contain the spread, while in 1978, it appears that all but one person in San Francisco has become a pod person. In both instances, it's too late. But in Kidman's *Invasion*, there aren't any pods. People are transforming into automatons as a result of disease, and the disease, it turns out, is reversible. So in the East Coast version, the story elements are softened. There's no alien invasion, and there's a happy ending. The really horrible outcomes of the story are reserved for the West Coast.

WE END WITH A QUESTION: Have our movies exported a style of California crime into mainstream America—that is, not just into movies but into American life in general? It could be said that there has always been senseless crime, and that the anarchists that beset the country (and the world) at the turn of the last century were practicing perversity and creating a sense of hopelessness long before the advent of the feature film. Obviously, no straight line can be drawn, no clean cause and effect. Yet one wonders if generations of films expressing senselessness—depicting crimes designed to create despair—have mainstreamed, as it were, this kind of crime to the extent that it has become a more frequent occurrence. It would be a jagged line and would have detours, but can we draw one all the same—one that connects from California's despair-inducing crime films to, say, the Manson murders and, from there, to the mass shootings that have become such a hideous feature of our national life?

It's impossible to say, because we're all in the same soup of culture—we're practically drowning in it—and thus can't tell what is causing what. In any case, the parallels are there.

CHAPTER NINE
Real Noir Is California Noir

Film noir has become a catch-all for a particular style of crime film that flourished in the 1940s and for most of the 1950s. It's characterized by black-and-white photography, long shadows, empty streets at night, and by the tendency of fate to just put the finger on a guy and mark him for senseless doom—and usually it *is* a guy. Women occupy this world, too, either as virtuous witnesses to a man's slide into hell or, just as often and most memorably, as amoral or willfully evil agents of destruction.

But despite a confluence of influences—hard-boiled detective fiction of the 1930s, German expressionist films of the 1920s, and the censorship that arrived in the mid-1930s and pretty much decreed that women could only be either all bad or all good—film noir is very much a California thing. It is a product of the aspirations and the lusts it inspires and the confusion and disappointment it generates.

This California product has been imported to every part of the world and has spawned countless imitators. There is New York noir, French noir, and Japanese noir, and in truth, almost every country has made noir films, for better and, with the notable exception of the French, mostly worse. But at their best, the moral scheme, the films' way of looking at life, comes from California—or more specifically from an outsider's fear of and attraction to the California way of life.

It's curious to think how, even when modern California was still a possession of Spain or (as of 1821) Mexico, California was already for Americans a place that offered the tempting alternative, where you could get away from everything you've ever been. The ancestors of these first white visitors had traveled to the East Coast of the United States from Europe in order to find religious freedom or escape religious oppression, so that they might express their Christianity in their own way. But now, here on the West Coast, their descendants were finding an escape from religion altogether.

Film noir—in its pure California strain—is in some way a response to this. In terms of its literary antecedents, it derives from the work of Raymond Chandler, Dashiell Hammett, and James M. Cain, none of whom were born here, but all of whom arrived here as young men and came of age as writers on California soil. They set most of their work in the state—mostly in Los Angeles, sometimes in San Francisco—and they depicted a world in which people behaved selfishly, often senselessly, and in which women constituted a threat. Both feared and celebrated, these women couldn't be resisted.

In this they presented a form of the same California drama that took place in earlier days, when the West Coast was still the frontier. Film noir heroes have their antecedents in those easterners who, tempted by the land, the climate, and the women, discarded the morality they grew up with, that had been part of the air they breathed all their lives. In its place, they embraced fun, even if it meant someday going to hell.

Film noir heroes operate in a more secular universe, but the parallels are clear. Over and over, we get the same message, expressed in deeds, though never overtly in words: *Sex can kill you, but it's worth it anyway.*

Thus, Robert Mitchum and Jane Greer, in the quintessential noir *Out of the Past* (1947), are reclining on the beach at night, somewhere in Mexico, and she tells him that she didn't steal the $40,000. He has been searching for her at the behest of a gangster, a man who should not be crossed. She implores, "Won't you believe me?" And Mitchum answers, "Baby, I don't care," and kisses her.

Of course, she stole the money. She's not even a good liar. But when he says, "Baby, I don't care," the audience loves it. The man is being a chump, an unbelievable idiot. He is wrecking his life—though this is Mitchum, who is cool enough to make this seem like a considered choice. But Mitchum or not, it's a remarkable thing that no one who watches that movie—not one person who has *ever* watched *Out of the Past* since it debuted in 1947—thinks, "Whatever you do, please don't kiss Jane Greer." No, we're rooting him on because we get the message, and we emphatically agree, even though we too have never quite said the words out loud: *Sex can kill you, but it's worth it anyway.*

THE EVIL WOMAN OF FILM NOIR—whether it's Jane Greer, Barbara Stanwyck (*Double Indemnity*), Audrey Totter (*Tension*), or any one of dozens—is in a sense a throwback to the late 1910s and very early 1920s, when it was implicitly forbidden to depict sexually active women as anything other than evil. Since movies had to have sex, the evil woman fit the bill. But the essential difference is that those early movies really did style themselves as cautionary tales. The women may have been alluring according to the fashion of the times, but their male victims were invariably pathetic, and the offscreen sex was nothing to envy. Sex could kill you, but it *wasn't* worth it, at least not then. But when a wave of censorship in the mid-1930s brought the evil woman back for a second time, this time in film noir, that's when the idea of enviable, ecstatic, life-enhancing, and life-destroying sex made its way into the movies.

Of course, when we're talking about sex as depicted in movies made during the forties and fifties—a period of rigid censorship—we're talking about something entirely in the realm of suggestion. In the early thirties, before the imposition of the Production Code, it was possible to show scenes that made it explicit that characters, even sympathetic characters, engaged in actual sex. We didn't see the sex, but we sometimes saw people on a bed, before the fade-out. There might be references to underwear scattered around the room. We might see people going home at night and then see them the next morning, having breakfast and wearing the same clothes. The fact of sex was usually made clear, and often there was no attempt to be subtle about it.

But with the imposition of censorship starting in mid-1934, such frankness was no longer possible, and noir itself, which rose up in the 1940s, can be seen as the perversion of natural impulse that inevitably resulted. If you could no longer show two people in a healthy sexual relationship, sex and romance had to become a little bit sick. If sex outside of marriage had to be punished, then a world had to be created in which the punishment at least made sense—that is, a context had to be created for the sex, the sickness, and the punishment. Thus, noir.

However, if there was actual sex in noir films, you just had to assume it. Sex couldn't be part of the drama. The eroticism in noir relations rather consists of the drama of initial seduction, which is sometimes synonymous with the drama of breaking a man's spirit, or at least his willpower, or at the very least his normal instinct for self-preservation. The men invariably end up damaged or broken, though it must be said that the women of noir usually don't fare well, either. *The Killers, Tension, The Maltese Falcon,* and *D.O.A.* end with the femme fatale heading to jail. In *Detour, Criss Cross, Out of the Past, The Lady from Shanghai, Scarlet Street, Double Indemnity, Gun Crazy, Too Late for Tears, Decoy, The Postman Always Rings Twice,* and *Murder, My Sweet,* and really too many other noirs to count, she ends up dead. Fate and a perverse universe drag down the men, while the women have to contend with all that, plus the censors who insisted that all evil had to be punished.

Yet the destructive women of noir weren't identical. They had in common the possession of a certain intense allure that could result in death, and yet within that broad definition, there was lots of room for variation. On the benign end of the spectrum we find Yvonne De Carlo in *Criss Cross* (1949), who just wants to get free of Dan Duryea, her menacing mobster lover. She sees Burt Lancaster as her ticket to freedom, and they both end up dead. But she's not a willful agent of destruction, nor is Joan

Bennett in *Scarlet Street* (1945), who is merely sloppy and self-indulgent and willing to go along with her boyfriend's criminal schemes. In their respective films, De Carlo and Bennett were, in a sense, simply relaxed and natural, and the movies were paranoid fantasies of what might happen to a man who became ensnared by temptation.

Most noir women were more actively amoral. They represent fantasies of a female sexuality completely divorced from the constraints of morality. They are male projections, and as such they can be thought of as misogynistic creations, but they were also fantasies of female power. And the attraction they hold for men in these films is the opportunity they offer of sex with a free woman—a completely free woman who is, at the very least, the man's equal. Yes, these women still have to exist in the world, and the world of these films is not stacked in a woman's favor, to be sure. But one on one, the woman can win.

What winning consists of, usually, is money. Barbara Stanwyck is sexy and greedy and has no morals at all in *Double Indemnity* (1944), enlisting a corruptible insurance man (Fred MacMurray) to kill her husband so she can collect a life insurance policy. And Ava Gardner is gorgeous and greedy enough in *The Killers* (1946) to sexually manipulate Burt Lancaster into committing a robbery—this, before stealing the money from him and plotting to have him killed.

Yet from early in the film noir cycle, the women in these movies became something more than examples of greed supercharged by amorality. There was something additional to their natures, something skewed. Audrey Totter in *Tension* (1949) leaves her husband (Richard Basehart), a perfectly nice pharmacist who is devoted to her, and then ends up killing the lover she left him for. In *Too Late for Tears* (1949), Lizabeth Scott is not just greedy but demented by greed. When she and her husband find $50,000 in a gangland drop-off, she persuades the husband not to turn the money over to the police. Soon, the gangster who missed the money shows up at her doorstep, but her avarice and ruthlessness are such that she ends up scaring *him*.

As for the case of *Out of the Past* and the $40,000 that Jane Greer takes, that's money stolen from gangster Kirk Douglas. Apparently, she also shot him, but after he recovers, he still wants her back. All her machinations, including the seduction of Robert Mitchum, are not for money, exactly, but for the precious commodity that money can buy—freedom. But in pursuit of this freedom, she becomes so single-minded that she kills three people. By the end of the film, half the attraction that she held for the audience has faded, as she has begun to look slightly mad.

But then, why shouldn't she go mad? These movies almost invariably invite us all to see the action from a male perspective, but if you imagine this very familiar story from the standpoint of Kathie, the character played by Greer, it becomes something else—the failed struggle of a woman to break free, using the only means she has at her disposal, which is her ability to seduce men who might help her to *become* free—she can't get there on her own. She's not thinking that sex is worth it even if it kills you. Rather, she's thinking that freedom is worth it, even if means risking joining a crowded cemetery that she herself has helped populate. But in a way that's just a corollary of the California idea—freedom, though expensive, is worth the risk.

Speaking of female perspective, *Born to Kill* (1947), set

mostly in San Francisco, did something unusual, perhaps unique: It reversed the sexes and thus created one of the more fascinating examples of the form. Claire Trevor played a socialite, who lives in wealthy splendor in San Francisco's Pacific Heights but has no money of her own. Her stepsister supports her. But she is on the verge of acquiring all the money she'll ever need, because she's engaged to a rich man in her sister's wealthy circle. So like most noir men, Trevor starts the film with a fairly stable life and with a willing, reasonable partner. The only thing she has to do is manage to not wreck things.

Trevor in *Born to Kill* is like a combination of the men and women that usually populate noir. Like noir's evil women, she has a streak of perversity. While on a trip to Reno to get divorced, she stumbles onto a gruesome murder scene, but, not wanting to get involved, she doesn't call the police but instead remains curiously detached, even though she knew one of the victims. Soon after, she figures out who the murderer is—a big, hard, brutish man with no discernible charm at all, played by Lawrence Tierney. But again, she fails to call the police because, of all things, she finds herself physically attracted to him. In this, she is like the noir men—she knows better but can't help herself.

Tierney follows her to San Francisco, where Trevor introduces this homicidal maniac to her sister, who begins dating him. Still, Trevor continues to see him on the side—not despite the fact that he is a murderer, but because he is. She has all the twistedness of a noir heroine and all the lunatic lust of a noir hero. She covers up his crimes—he continues to kill people—and eventually he kills her, and then the police kill him. Trevor remains, to the end, a sympathetic figure, in the same way that noir men do. She takes one wrong step in the direction of sexual impulse, and then events gradually spiral out of control and drag her down with them. It's not a happy ending, but there's no question that the outcome of *Born to Kill* restores the moral order, with all the blameless people unharmed and, in fact, left safer than before. In this, it is typical of most film noir set in San Francisco: The characters pretty much get what they deserve— and avoid getting what they don't deserve.

CALIFORNIA NOIR IS NOIR IN ITS TRUEST STRAIN. Like bourbon actually made in Kentucky, Champagne from Champagne, and Burgundy from Burgundy, California noir is the real stuff. But just as Burgundy and Champagne have, within them, different regions with different virtues, California noir has two prime locations, San Francisco and Los Angeles. Each city produces a distinct noir varietal, though there's no need to overstate this. Of course, there's overlap. There are some San Francisco noirs that feel more like Los Angeles noir, and vice versa. There are also noirs that take place in both cities. Still, the differences— the tendencies of each type of noir—are real and worth exploring.

As photographic entities, both cities are beautiful, and being beautiful, they convey the California idea that here is a place so lovely that people must make their *own* problems. And people do. Even divorced from the ugliness, bad weather, miserable atmosphere, and strategic difficulty of navigating life that we find in *other* cities, people in film noir find the means to screw up their lives in catastrophic ways. Yet there's a difference in the beauty of San Francisco and Los Angeles and what that beauty means on screen.

In film, San Francisco represents a pristine ideal: You may be having a rotten time, but the city is perfectly fine. In *Out of the Past*, Robert Mitchum takes time off from watching his life circle the drain to ask Rhonda Fleming if she has ever been to New York. When she says no, he tells her, "You take a trip there one time. You'll find out why I'm in San Francisco."

For the movies, San Francisco is like a pure essence, sometimes a moral rebuke, sometimes an impervious ideal, against which the impurity, perfidy, or unhappiness of the characters can stand out in sharper relief. In *Vertigo* (1958), Alfred Hitchcock used it as a rather amazing place to stage a nervous breakdown. Set in New York, it could not have been the same movie, because in New York *everybody* is having a nervous breakdown. But in San Francisco he's all alone.

In *D.O.A.* (1949), Edmond O'Brien walks around Market Street, sweating and panicking, suffering from a slow-acting poison, but the city just goes on behind him and in front of him. San Francisco isn't *happy* that O'Brien is going to drop dead in the next few hours. It's just too beautiful to get worked up about it.

This brings us to a key difference between San Francisco and Los Angeles in the movies. San Francisco doesn't care if you live or die. But Los Angeles? Los Angeles *wants* to kill you.

L.A.'s beauty is the beauty of illusion. Its beauty is the face that the devil shows you for the sake of luring you in. And then the head slowly spins around and there are worms coming out of its eyes. It's not something phony that's hiding something dark and true. Rather, it's something irresistible and empty that's hiding the true depths, implications, and consequences of its emptiness.

San Francisco is Olympian, disinterested. L.A. tempts you— that is, you the movie protagonist—with everything you know you shouldn't want but do—pool parties, sex with strangers, indolence, unearned status. In the history of cinema, there has never been a Hollywood party presented on screen in which any protagonist ever had fun. Yet we always wish we were invited! And then, just when you're on the hook, the trap is sprung. Once you're trapped, Los Angeles makes you pay and pay.

Even in a film noir context, the moral universe of San Francisco most often makes sense. In *The Maltese Falcon* (1941), from a story by Dashiell Hammett, Brigid O'Shaughnessy (Mary Astor) is a very bad person, but every place has one. On a foggy night, she lures Miles Archer (Jerome Cowan) into an alley and kills him, but by the end, Sam Spade (Humphrey Bogart) solves the case and tells her: "You're taking the fall." As she should.

Orson Welles's *The Lady from Shanghai* (1947) introduces a group of wealthy sharks, all with a blood lust to devour each other. But then they do—and somehow manage to devour no one else. Everett Sloane and Rita Hayworth turn an amusement park hall of mirrors into a shooting gallery. Both end up dead, but the one almost-innocent bystander—the Irishman played by Welles himself—walks away with barely a flesh wound. In a Los Angeles noir, he could have easily been killed, too, or better yet, he would have been executed for their murder.

One of the most seductive and mad of femme fatales is the relatively unknown Jean Gillie in the film *Decoy* (1946). She played a woman obsessed with a buried treasure. Her bank-robbing boyfriend is in prison, and she is desperate to get a map to where he buried the money. Along the way, she kills several people and thoroughly enjoys it. She kicks the jack out from under a car, causing it to collapse on a man underneath it, and laughs.

But *Decoy* is told in flashback, as the evil woman's deathbed confession. And though she's evil to the end—at one point she pretends at contrition in order to trick a cop into showing some sympathy, then she laughs in his face—the end does come. San Francisco gets to go back to being San Francisco. There was an evil person living there, sure, but now she's gone, and isn't that good? Now everyone can relax again.

A typical example of San Francisco noir is *Dark Passage* (1947), in which convicted wife murderer Humphrey Bogart escapes from San Quentin and is taken in by Lauren Bacall. She lets him stay in her nice Montgomery Street apartment because she has a hunch that he's innocent, and what do you know? He is. And not only that, he proves it to her, and they live happily ever after, albeit outside the United States. In San Francisco noir, the world can make sense.

In Los Angeles noir, the whole point is that the world does *not* make sense. In fact, it's almost as if everything is made subordinate to that assertion, so that the story becomes secondary. Every movie becomes a quiet scream: Something is terribly wrong.

IT HAS BECOME A COMMONPLACE in noir studies to say that the rise of film noir is related to the detonation of the two atomic bombs that ended World War II, and to the nuclear arms race that followed. In this way, the nihilism of noir becomes an expression of the existential terror inherent in people's belief that civilization was on borrowed time and that humanity would soon destroy itself.

But this has always struck me as the worst sort of *post hoc ergo propter hoc* reasoning. Not only would one occurrence not necessarily be caused by the other—and not only does this kind of argument not account for all the many innocuous Hollywood genres that flourished in the same era—but even the *timing* (the *post hoc* part of the argument) is wrong. Film noir was already full blown by 1944 with *Double Indemnity*, a year before Hiroshima and Nagasaki, and the nuclear arms race didn't fully set in until August of 1949, when the Soviet Union got the bomb, at which point the philosophical undertone of noir was already firmly established. After all, Americans weren't worried about us blowing up *other* people but about other people blowing up *us*.

Instead, the philosophical underpinnings of noir are the products of Los Angeles, of the confusion and alienation that that city instills in the human soul.

New York is always talked about as the city of the new, the city that is never completely finished, that is always under construction. But every New Yorker is aware of the city's history and feels its presence. Even a tourist walking for twenty minutes in downtown Manhattan will stumble onto the spot where George Washington gave the first inaugural address or see, in the narrow streets around Wall Street, the suggestion of an old New York of horses and buggies. Everywhere in New York, there is a presence of history, of some life that went before.

Los Angeles has a history, but aside from the foot- and handprints outside Grauman's and the names along Hollywood Boulevard—themselves monuments to the ephemeral nature of fame and to the ultimate fate of secular deities—it is a city of the present tense. Even more than that, it's a city that negates the past as irrelevant. So there can really be no comfort in anything but the Now, and not even a conviction that the Now has any intrinsic value, because today's Now will soon be tomorrow's Then. It is a city that whispers in your ear, "This is it," and that makes you feel, "This isn't enough."

An environment that's all about Now and all about surfaces, one that evokes no faith in anything of deeper value, or of anything mysterious beyond the vagaries of cruel luck, will itself create the sense of a godless universe with no future—no need for an atomic bomb here. The writers and filmmakers of noir were already on that page long before the Enola Gay. This L.A. feeling, at its worst, connects with our fear of futility and isolation, the sense that our lives are pointless, that we can't win, that we never could, that we don't matter. That is the modern disease, and noir, at its truest, expresses it.

Ever since the term *film noir* came into use, there have been arguments about how to define it and questions as to which films can be classified under that label. Noir is a look, an attitude, a genre, an era, and a style, and you can shove this or that movie under its umbrella if you make a reasonable case. But if we are to narrow our point of focus to the most potent expressions of the form, we are talking about a philosophy and a view of life as well. We are talking about the confusion, despair, and resignation that Los Angeles brought into the mix.

That is the best noir, the real noir, the Châteauneuf-du-Pape noir, of light reflecting off rain-slicked streets, and crazy, awful things happening that make no sense. In Nicholas Ray's *In a Lonely Place* (1950), Humphrey Bogart makes the acquaintance of a friendly hatcheck girl and the next day finds out she was brutally murdered that same night. He barely reacts, which counts against him in our eyes, but *we* barely react ourselves, except to acknowledge that this sometimes happens. In *The Postman Always Rings Twice* (1946), lovers Lana Turner and John Garfield, driven by lust and greed, fake an accident and ultimately get away with the murder of her husband. But then just when they're in the clear, they get into a legitimate car accident, in which she's killed, and he ends up going to the chair for her murder. This is not a case of the moral order restored but of a malevolent universe trying to be funny.

In *Sunset Boulevard* (1950), a former silent film star rebels against the Los Angeles truth that the past means nothing, and so she becomes violent and delusional. But noir enlists us into its ethos, because we agree with the world that Norma Desmond means nothing, and we remain unmoved even when she carts out a film of her younger self—real footage of a luminous Gloria Swanson in the 1928 film *Queen Kelly.*

The power of Los Angeles noir is that we half believe its view on things because we live in the modern world, too, and because we've internalized so much of the city's ethos from the movies we've consumed. We're like spiritual cousins of Dan Duryea in *Black Angel* (1946), who spends the entire movie looking to solve a murder, only to discover that he himself did it, while blackout drunk.

Noir would have no power, no resonance, and could make no connection if we didn't fear the cold implications of the modernity that noir and Los Angeles express. In noir, we wake up to the nightmare that follows our seduction.

It's a world in which God doesn't matter—or worse, has decided that *we* don't.

CHAPTER TEN
Natural Disaster

The love-hate relationship that California has with the rest of the country reaches its orgasmic culmination in the prospect of all the beautiful people falling into the sea.

It's terrifying and hilarious, this version of the California myth reconstructed for a bitter East Coast, for a population that spends three months out of every year shoveling snow. These are people who have to buy items such as aerosol de-icers, things most California natives have never even heard of. They have to buy gloves, and not as a fashion accessory. And even as they're doing these unpleasant things, they can't help but remember the people they know who left town for California, who went to the West Coast thinking they were better and prettier . . . because they *were*.

Oh, the thought of these escapees, sitting in the sun, having umbrella drinks, picking oranges off of trees, voting for Democrats, feeling privileged yet virtuous, and disgustingly pleased with themselves. It's nothing less than unbearable . . . until the happy thought comes that these escapees will not be ultimately repudiated by the small scare of failure. No, they will experience a comeuppance practically Mel Brooksian. God will actually take that whole chunk of the country and plunge it into the ocean. And with that happy thought, frozen East Coasters get a warm feeling as they take their plastic scrapers and try to get the ice off the windshield. Yes, they think, we're better off right here.

If you live in California, you end up hearing a lot about other people's weather, usually on the news. Sub-zero temperatures, snowdrifts, cars floating down the street. You hear about disastrous hurricanes and tornadoes as well, but most of the bad weather is of the awful but pedestrian variety, seasonable and predictable.

In the California of popular imagination, there are no seasons, and the disasters are not predictable, and their very unpredictability makes them more cinematic in that, until disaster strikes, everything usually seems wonderful. Everything seems little-do-they-know. And incidentally, this variety of California wonderful is not merely for the rich and the lucky. On the contrary, you can live in a studio apartment in a little enclave in Daly City and walk to the beach and feel that the world is yours.

Earthquakes and, more recently, forest fires are the twin terrors of the California imagination, but of the two, earthquakes are the more mysterious and random and can't be fought, and thus they're the most mythic and frightening. Californians deal with them the way human beings deal with most ongoing threats. They don't think about them! Yet even when we're not thinking about them, they're never that far from the surface. Someone kicks the bed, a truck rumbles up the street, and the thought crosses the mind, Is this an earthquake?

In fact, it almost never is, not because earthquakes are rare but because when it's an earthquake, you don't have to ask. It's amazing how fast you know. Here's the difference, for the uninitiated: When something is shaking in relationship to something else remaining still, that is *not* an earthquake. In an earthquake, even a small earthquake, *everything* is shaking, and shaking yet more in reaction to everything else shaking. It is an experience of shaking feeding on shaking, and it's literally and figuratively destabilizing, such that the feeling of being unable to trust the solid ground stays around for days until, once again, the welcome illusion of complete and utter safety returns.

One has to wonder what it must have been like for those very first transplanted Easterners who established themselves in an earthly paradise only to get the shaky punch line months or years down the line. It must have been a rude shock indeed, a case of good news/bad news akin to marrying the ideal spouse who is perfect in every way except that he or she just might kill you in your sleep. Sure, they probably won't, but they might without warning. Still, don't worry, because even if it happens, it probably won't happen for years and years and years, and maybe not even *then*. Except it *could* happen in the next minute. In the meantime, just relax and don't give it a second thought.

EARTHQUAKE MOVIES OFFER the unlimited possibility of spectacle— anything can be destroyed in an earthquake movie and in any conceivable way. They also offer story satisfaction because we, as spectators, have an advantage over everyone in the movie. We know what's coming. The people on screen don't. And so, we have the pleasure of watching and waiting for them to catch on to what we already know.

Most people, when they imagine a good story, don't think of this. When they imagine sitting in a theater and being riveted to their seat with wonder and expectation, they picture themselves trying to figure out what will happen next. They expect a story constructed as a series of revelations. Yet it's often just as effective to let an audience know exactly what's about to happen and then present the plot as a series of situations in which the characters find out what the audience already knows.

To a large extent, this is how disaster movies function. They often begin on some observation station, located in a remote outpost, where a technician, on a routine night, looks at a computer terminal and says, "Oh. My. God." That exact scene eventually became a cliché in movies, but it became one because it was effective and satisfying enough to be repeated again and again. The audience knows the disaster is coming. The audience has the fun of seeing one person realize it. And then the audience looks forward to a series of further scenes in which more people realize what's happening; until, finally, President Morgan Freeman gets the bad news in the Oval Office. Interestingly, this is often the most enjoyable part of any disaster movie. Once everybody knows, there's less to look forward to.

This way of telling stories is not confined to movies. Rather, movies are replicating something that human beings do naturally. This is how we tell our *own* disaster stories, as a series of realizations. And for dramatic effect, we do our best to break down those realizations into their finest particles.

Some real-life disasters lend themselves better than others to that mode of storytelling. The terrorist attack of 9/11, for example, is always told as a series of realizations—what we thought when the first plane hit, what we realized when the second plane hit, what we felt when we heard about the Pentagon, followed by the horror of the first building coming down, followed by the anticipation *and* horror of the second building coming down. Everyone's 9/11 story is told in this way. It's a bad 9/11 story that begins and ends with the person waking up and finding out that the whole thing has happened already.

Even when a story doesn't fit quite so neatly into that step-by-step structure, the structure of step-by-step revelation is usually imposed onto it. Find someone old enough to remember the JFK assassination, and they'll tell you about hearing the first bulletin, then about hearing that the president was shot in the head, then hearing about the priests (having delivered the last rites) *saying* that he was dead, followed by the announcement ("apparently official") from Walter Cronkite on CBS or Robert MacNeil on NBC.

In a similar way, in more recent times, you may sometimes hear Democrats say, "We were having a party. And at first she was winning. And then they said Wisconsin was too close to call, and then Pennsylvania started looking funny, and then they said something about Michigan . . ."

This human tendency to tell stories as a series of realizations can be found even in the way people talk about that most sudden of disasters, the earthquake: "At first I thought it was the construction next door, then I realized it was an earthquake, then I ran to the doorframe, then I realized the earthquake wasn't stopping—it was getting worse—so I dove under the table, and that's when it stopped."

Having experienced realization, we love to inflict realization on others. Back in the day, before smartphone news alerts meant everyone finds out everything at the same time, it used to be possible to surprise friends with tidbits of semi-disastrous information. It hardly needs mention that death was everyone's particular favorite. If you happened to be the first to hear that a celebrity died, it was always fun to call whoever liked the celebrity best to inflict the realization and see how he or she reacted. It was like being a newscaster and a sadist combined, i.e., the best of both worlds.

ONE OF THE IMPLICIT IDEAS of all disaster films is that whatever happened, you probably deserved it. We weren't unified enough, so the space aliens came to conquer us. We were too violent, so the space aliens needed to impose order. We relied too much on computers, and so the computers took over. We believed too much in machines, and so we hit an iceberg. We didn't care about climate change, so now the whole north of the United States is covered in ice. We couldn't live in peace, and so we knocked over the Statue of Liberty and the apes took over everything. Behind every disaster movie is an invisible scold, waving a finger at the people eating popcorn and saying, "You. Yes, *you*, idiot. *You* did this. It's your own damn fault."

As for California disaster movies, they're often based on the idea that California just pressed its luck by being too beautiful, or that its people pushed it too far by being too carefree, or too happy, or not guilt-ridden enough, or too sinful, or simply for being amazingly stupid enough to live in an earthquake zone. Since most of these movies are made in California, it's hard to say whether they're made to titillate Californians or satisfy non-Californians about their life choices. It's probably a combination of both. They're certainly *enjoyed* by both—by all kinds of people all over the world, though I must admit there's a special frisson in watching a movie like *San Andreas* while sitting on the San Andreas fault.

San Francisco (1936), the classic earthquake movie, spends about eighty minutes of screen time explaining why San Francisco in 1906 deserved to be leveled. The filmmakers aren't exactly happy that it happened, but with all those brothels, and the infidelity, and the Barbary Coast . . . If only to get Jeanette MacDonald to stop singing, the Earth had to intervene.

Though earthquakes are very much a part of the experience of all Californians, the 1906 quake made earthquakes not merely a part of San Francisco history, but of legend. The legend remains to this day, but it was especially fresh in the pre–World War II era. In films such as *San Francisco* and *Frisco Jenny* (1932), San Franciscans are portrayed with extra respect, as resilient survivors. It's rather like the way Americans, to this day, think of Londoners in terms of the heroism their grandparents showed during the blitz.

But all this history should not obscure the more pressing fact that California, with a special emphasis on San Francisco, has become a particular locus for disaster films of recent years. These films can be understood fully only when placed in the context of national cinematic trends since January 1, 2000—or, to be more precise, since September 11, 2001.

The turn of the millennium found the United States in a particularly strong and confident position, without any powerful enemies, enjoying a booming economy, and with the Internet and all its possibilities suddenly opening before us. The era was so placid that there was time for reflection. Serious American movies focused on heroines out of Jane Austen and Henry James, as if in search of feminist forebears or perhaps out of desire to contemplate the gains that women had made over the course of the century. Meanwhile, there was a trend in films about World War II, as if times were so peaceful that Hollywood needed to import strife and conflict from other generations.

The 9/11 attacks were a profound shock that discombobulated America's sense of self, sense of safety, and belief in the permanence of its structures and institutions. Television screens were full of images of civic chaos. Suddenly, the idea entered the collective mind that everything we thought was solid and immovable was actually fragile, that civilization was delicate and civility a veneer. Any shock, if big enough, might topple us into an unprotected state.

Since then, one of the major themes and spectacles of Hollywood cinema has been civic catastrophe. The other two themes have been alien invasion and the fear of artificial intelligence—of computers taking over. All three bespeak a sense of impermanence, of tentativeness, of a lack of faith and a dread of the future. A people who turned on the television and found themselves smack in a new world now found themselves attracted to and titillated by the thing they feared most—of everything good suddenly going away and everything horrible happening in a flash.

Of course, there were sci-fi disaster movies before 9/11. *Independence Day*, the number one box office movie of 1996, combined elements of both civic chaos and alien invasion and featured the destruction of every national landmark, including the White House. But the pre-9/11 disaster movies were less frequent, and when they did exist, they tended to be more benign and straightforward. *Twister*, for example, the number two box office movie of 1996, was all about researchers chasing tornadoes. The tornadoes were trouble. They were scary, and they were destructive. But they weren't *trying* to destroy our way of life. They weren't consciously malevolent entities, and they could be relied upon to eventually go away on their own.

That San Francisco has become a particular epicenter for cinematic disaster in the post-9/11 era is largely to do with the Golden Gate Bridge. As an indelible landmark, it has no equivalent in Los Angeles—all L.A. has is that famous white building, but no one knows what it is. (It's City Hall.) There's the Hollywood sign, but if a sign collapses, who gets hurt? And how much would it cost to rebuild? The Golden Gate Bridge, meanwhile, has few equivalents within the entire United States. New Orleans is a great city, but it has no easily identifiable landmark. How about the Willis Tower in Chicago? Did you even know it's now called the Willis Tower? Didn't you think it was called the Sears Tower? And can you even picture it? Perhaps you can picture the Gateway Arch in St. Louis. That's a good one, but come on. The Golden Gate Bridge is a landmark of a different order.

The bridge is up there with the Empire State Building, the Statue of Liberty, the U.S. Capitol building, and the White House.

It is as internationally identifiable as the Arc de Triomphe and the Eiffel Tower in Paris, the Colosseum in Rome, the Leaning Tower of Pisa in Italy, and the pyramids in Egypt. And why does it keep getting destroyed in the post-9/11 era? Answer: It's America's most identifiable landmark that's contained in a city that wasn't attacked in September of 2001.

Put simply, filmmakers can't show the Empire State Building getting destroyed without making audiences remember the World Trade Center. They can't show the White House getting obliterated without evoking memories of the crash of Flight 93, which was headed there before the passengers revolted. But showing the Golden Gate Bridge getting destroyed tickles that fear without reminding people of the specific nightmare they're trying to gain mastery over. The goal of a blockbuster, after all, is to generate a sense of omnipotence, that of watching death and destruction from a godlike remove—rather like a psychiatric patient facing paralyzing fears and mentally playing out dreaded scenarios as a way of overcoming an anxiety disorder. But the patient that is the American audience can never gain mastery if suddenly plunged into a specific memory of past trauma. That would be too close.

Of course, depictions of the bridge's destruction are not new to the twenty-first century. Bridge attacks go back at least as far as *It Came from Beneath the Sea* (1955). San Francisco is a vivid place, and even once the bridge is disposed of, it remains a target-rich environment (Alcatraz, Coit Tower). What we're talking about now is an *increase* in attacks, something that, for a time in recent history, became a recurrent staple of summer.

For the record, the bridge was damaged or destroyed in four

movies from 2009 alone (*Mega Shark Versus Giant Octopus*, *Monsters vs. Aliens*, *Terminator Salvation*, and *Land of the Lost*). It was shown already ruined in *The Book of Eli* (2010). It was damaged by rampaging apes in *Rise of the Planet of the Apes* (2011). In 2013, all of downtown was damaged in *Star Trek Into Darkness*, and the bridge was destroyed in *Pacific Rim*. *Godzilla* did a number on the bridge the following year, and it was destroyed again in both *Terminator Genisys* and *San Andreas* in 2015.

Since then, things have calmed down a bit as far as San Francisco is concerned, but the national trend of depicting civic chaos has become a regular feature of Marvel Comics movies, which regularly show violence spreading out into suburban and city streets, with catastrophic physical damage being done to buildings. These depictions haven't stopped or slowed down.

Such scenes of destruction have become so common in our films that we barely notice it. We take it all for granted, as though this were a reasonable and expected thing, that every summer Hollywood should flood the world with images of our cities and landmarks getting destroyed.

But for a moment, consider this: Imagine if half the movies coming out of France showed the Eiffel Tower getting destroyed, or Paris streets getting ripped up and smashed by fights between superheroes or highly powerful mutants. Imagine if every other British film saw Big Ben and Parliament getting trashed. Imagine if half the films out of Italy had the Leaning Tower finally toppling, pushed over by the hand of a monster.

Now imagine all these movies happening, again and again, for a period of *years*. What conclusions might you draw about the collective mentality of such a people—of a people disseminating and celebrating visions of their own obliteration? Would you think, Oh, well, obviously these folks consider themselves omnipotent and they're just having fun with these outlandish fantasies? I doubt it. I think you would surmise that something is seriously wrong with the nation producing such visions, that its inhabitants' confidence is nonexistent, their mental health suspect, their mood both depressed and delusional, and their vision of the future bleak. You would think this is a nation in trouble. Moreover, you would expect that such a country would run into a crisis, and soon.

Just as a person who is terrified of heights sometimes must fight a perverse impulse to jump, people will sometimes desire the thing they fear, if only to get the worst over with—hence, the trend of *post*apocalyptic movies, too many to count. If movies really are how a culture dreams, then what are we to make of a culture whose current dream is of itself being crushed and annihilated? And what do we make of the dreamers sitting in audiences, stuffing their faces and laughing at the prospect?

No, the function of these films is not about overcoming fear, at least not in an intelligent or empathetic way. They may cater to the impulse to overcome fear, but their business model is based on perpetuating and spreading it. These are fantasies of nihilism, in which an audience becomes willing to contemplate its own destruction so long as everything else is ruined, too.

In the middle of the 2010s, I'd look at Godzilla rampaging through San Francisco and wonder what it meant and what it portended. Years later, I think I understand. The fear of extraterrestrials is the disguised fear of illegal aliens; the fear of artificial intelligence is the disguised fear of automation and job loss; the fear of the apocalypse is the disguised fear of terrorism. And the spectacle of destruction these films offer is the comforting spectacle of identifying with the destroyer and thus no longer having to worry.

Or to put it another way, the monster stomping through our cities, the monster that kept recurring in other forms, the monster that made us wonder why he was being conjured by our collective unconscious, the monster whose meaning and portent was always a tantalizing mystery, has now been revealed. What an awesome thing to realize that those films of the mid-decade were predicting the nation's immediate political future.

DISASTER MOVIES USUALLY EXIST in relation to one of the four elements. *Airport* (1970), about a plane trying to land after being damaged by a bomb, began a cycle of 1970s large-cast disaster films. That film, which was set mostly in the air, was followed by the watery disaster movie *The Poseidon Adventure* (1972), a Christian parable set on a capsized ocean liner. By 1974, the genre was so popular that there were two California-based disaster movies, the earth-based *Earthquake*, set in Los Angeles and released in November; and the fire-based *Towering Inferno*, set in San Francisco and released in December. Once the four elements had exhausted themselves, the genre petered out—but in a blaze of glory.

Occasionally, disaster movies revive, and when they do, we once again encounter the destructive capacities of these elements. *Twister*, about tornadoes, fits into the "air" category— angry air, but air all the same. So, in their way, did *Contagion*

(2011), partly filmed in San Francisco, and *Outbreak* (1995), mostly filmed in Southern California. In those films, the air was poisonous with lethal viruses. No one—at least no germophobe (and by now, aren't we all?)—can ever forget the movie theater scene in *Outbreak*. Some infected person coughs in the back of the theater and we see an animated version of the virus going into the mouths of various laughing spectators. In times of plague, never attend a comedy.

Along this line, it seems inevitable that the real-life coronavirus pandemic will be the subject of multiple movies, and, if past is prologue, not all of them will be disaster films. Indeed, probably most of them won't be; instead they will be dramas telling the stories of scientific breakthroughs. Perhaps some or all of these will contain rapturous scenes, showing a convulsion of human happiness not seen since V-J Day. I imagine people once again sitting in packed theaters, while delirious scenes play out on screen, of vaccinated sailors and vaccinated nurses whipping off their masks and kissing on Hollywood Boulevard or San Francisco's Market Street—or Times Square. At least that's a happy thought as this book goes to press.

But to get back to those seventies movies: *The Towering Inferno* is all about hubris. What could possibly go wrong when so many rich people get together to build a skyscraper? What could go wrong if they cut corners and don't install the proper sprinklers or use safe materials that won't go up like a rag dipped in turpentine? Though there are dated elements, *The Towering Inferno* retains much of the appeal it had in its own day because we instantly recognize the characters, as if they are stock figures in a morality play.

The good guys are the working class, the makers and doers versus the suits, the bean counters, and the society players. *The Towering Inferno* tells us to value hard detail over abstraction and profiteering, to value the details of engineering that go into the making of a sound building. The people who can make a building stand are the unseen titans of the world, the debunkers of the upside-down notion that money equals virtue.

As for *Earthquake* (1974), it's worth remembering that one of the recurrent and satisfying images of medieval art is the hellmouth. The gaping threat to the crust of the Earth itself is spiritually primal. Such visions were a way for pagan qualities of disbelief to be quelled by elemental threats: Hell is down below, and that's where you're going if you don't straighten out.

Curiously, the movies use these elements in their raw form. The Old Testament might take these disasters as a cue to create order within society and the spirit, but in California disaster movies, we just get the raw material from which all myth and religion came. In *Earthquake*, the dogs go crazy in advance of the event, their animal intuition tuned to what will happen, and we gaze critically at the houses built on skinny stilts and wonder what the builders were thinking. Were they stupid? Overly optimistic? Arrogant? Or did they simply know that the checks would be cashed and that they'd be halfway across the continent before the Big One hit?

San Andreas (2015), which came some forty years later, will probably remain for some time the ultimate California earthquake film. First, it's not really about the much anticipated Big One but rather about a series of Big Ones. They never stop. They start at Hoover Dam and work their way up the map, as seismologist Paul Giamatti gets more and more frantic with his Cassandra-like powers of prognostication: "I cannot emphasize this enough to the people of San Francisco," he says in a television interview. "You need to get out. And I mean now." And obviously the best route is to the north, right over the Golden Gate Br—

Uh-oh.

San Andreas is not the kind of movie that gets taken seriously, but it's an elegant, fun disaster film with a secure sense of style. It's not satire, but the knowingness of the performances— notably those of Giamatti and Dwayne ("The Rock") Johnson, who plays a rescue worker, keep it just outside the boundaries of comedy. The Hoover Dam crumbles, Los Angeles is wrecked, and smaller cities are reduced to punchy anecdotes. ("Bakersfield. Or what's left of it.") Best and worst of all, San Francisco is turned into Venice. The streets disappear and turn into water—a tourist destination to be sure, if they can ever drag the bodies out.

EARTHQUAKE MOVIES USUALLY have a moral element to them. The earthquake is obviously no one's fault, but there is always someone in the movie to illustrate human selfishness or shortsightedness, someone who lacks the optimal human qualities that the crisis calls for, someone who pursues their own self-interest and ends up dead, and there often will be just a hint that more people would survive if people didn't have these qualities.

There's also the suggestion that those who rise to the moment will be better for the experience, which is always the goal in California—self-actualization, this time through disaster.

CHAPTER ELEVEN
Utopia

Once photography was invented, everything from Abraham Lincoln on was in black-and-white. The surrounding world was in color, but black-and-white was the world of memory, the world of photos and, later, the world of movies.

This state of affairs existed for over a hundred years. Then, in a span of a year or two, the world changed. The black-and-white cover of the Beatles' *Revolver* (1966) was followed by the color cover of the Beatles' *Sgt. Pepper's Lonely Hearts Club Band* (1967). Barbara Eden in *I Dream of Jeannie* was black-and-white in the beginning of 1966, then turned into living-color Barbara Eden in the fall of 1966.

This change plays itself into the iconography and mythology of the 1960s. The early 1960s—like the fifties and forties—are in black-and-white, but the middle to late sixties see an explosion of glorious color. This change, a technological thing, in retrospect feels as if it had a philosophical or attitudinal component, as if the moment of that switch had something to do with some extra exhilaration in the air. It's as if a change had taken place in the world itself, with color just reflecting that reality. And few movies convey that sense of a world changing—suddenly bursting into vividness, beauty, and possibility—more than *Monterey Pop* (1968), D. A. Pennebaker's documentary about the music festival that took place over three days in June 1967.

The festival was arranged by John Phillips of the Mamas and the Papas, whose "California Dreaming" was performed there. He also wrote the song "San Francisco," as a way of assuring locals that the festival would be peaceful, or should we say "pacific"? Sung by Scott McKenzie, it was released in May of 1967 and by the first week of June, it was the number four song in the country. It became the theme song—and invitation—for people from all over the country to come to San Francisco for the festival, though when they got to San Francisco, they might have been surprised to find out they still had to do a three-hour drive to get to Monterey.

To see *Monterey Pop* is to be reminded how California defines itself for each generation as the gold at the end of the American rainbow, the place of Utopia, the place to dream about from the other side of the country—those unlucky places where the leaves are brown and the skies turn gray. As the dream of every iconoclast who wants to find fellow iconoclasts who are iconoclastic in *exactly the same way*, California provides the ideal feeling of uniqueness and togetherness at the same time.

The Monterey we see on screen is a place where a mistreated underdog and lifelong misfit can finally become Janis Joplin before the eyes of the world, and an already famous Cass Elliot, sitting in the front row, can watch in jaw-dropped awe. And somehow, seeing the movie years later, it doesn't quite mar the moment to be aware that in less than a decade both of these talented young women would be dead, and that one would be a casualty of the very music scene being celebrated in this documentary. It doesn't mar the moment because, film being film, they'll never be dead to *us*; and California being California, they seem to exist in a world of eternal youth, where death is no issue.

Thus, even knowing what we know, the film instills a feeling of a utopia being created, of some ideal distillation of values being possible, and just around the corner. Everyone is beautiful, stars and audience alike. Everyone is happy. Everyone is in harmony, and nothing bad can happen. It is just possible that from now on, everyone will either look like Michelle Phillips or like someone Michelle Phillips could be in love with, and the temperature will always be in the mid-70s with a light breeze. The future is as bright as the colors people are wearing.

But as is so often the case in life, it's at precisely the moment when things seem as if they can only get better that they are at their best point.

UTOPIAS NEVER LAST. In fact, as California movies tell us, they never really happen, and the quest can lead straight to hell. And even when they don't, the dream fades. It can't be held.

Gidget, which I alluded to in chapter two, is a 1959 film with Sandra Dee that is rather unappreciated today, largely because people who don't bother to see it assume it should be lumped together with some of the sillier beach movies that were made in the years that followed. But some dated moments aside—if

Gidget's mother were any more lobotomized, she'd be a Stepford Wife—it's a gently compelling film about a young woman's coming-of-age and about the allure of the beach and the coast. It's about the desires that California makes seem possible, and the dream that you could build a life made up entirely of wonder, with no drudgery.

In an early scene, Gidget goes with friends on a "manhunt" to the beach, looking for guys. But Gidget is not as boy crazy as her friends. In fact, her best friend, to modern eyes, seems as though she might be a lesbian, and Gidget herself doesn't express much interest in sex. When she goes to the beach, what arrests her imagination isn't the male surfers but the actual surfing. Her friends go their way, but Gidget winds up spending the summer on the beach, first becoming a kind of mascot to these fellows and then becoming one of them. She buys her own surfboard and begins to take lessons and starts surfing with the guys.

In this group of surfers, the most important is a man known as Kahuna. He appears to be in his thirties—he's played by Cliff Robertson—and for years, this Kahuna has done nothing but chase the waves. He lives in a makeshift beach hut, and this is just one stop on a circuit that takes him as far as Hawaii. All this, of course, makes him exotic to the young men in his circle. James Darren played Moondoggie, who is scheduled to start college in the fall, but he wants to be like Kahuna. He doesn't want to conform. It's 1959, and already there's a whiff of the sixties on the ocean air. He wants to chuck his college plans and make his life an endless summer.

The power of the movie is contained in its backdrop, the beach world that's natural and physical. The movie creates the sense that there are beach towns all the way down the coast, a chain of them, presenting limitless places for wanderlust. Here, finally, is a place on the same scale as imagination, as grand as youth and lust and as limitless as time seems to an eighteen-year-old. Coming into their own just at the period of life when society starts slowly applying the handcuffs, here's this place that says that life doesn't have to be constrained. And so, as the movie goes along, the bodies get browner and browner and seem to blend in with the wood and the sand.

The movie makes us very aware that Gidget is becoming a woman and beginning to have sexual feelings. At one point she throws herself at Kahuna, presumably with the idea of losing her virginity. He decides to scare her off by playing along, then realizes that he's beginning to get aroused and throws her out before anything happens. But because Moondoggie doesn't understand what's happening, he ends up breaking with Kahuna, and the summer idyll falls apart, just in time for the new school year.

Kahuna is a distinct character, a sort of Prince Hamlet off to the side of the film, a complicated, decent, and moody figure, someone with an underlying sorrow, who is trying to make sense of life and get through it without creating any more damage. Apparently, he was in the Korean War and the experience scarred him. Through Cliff Robertson's performance, we understand the price of a rootless life, that nonattachment has costs, just as attachment does. And that all these choices, attachment or nonattachment, require courage.

If *Gidget* were made ten years later, it would have had a different ending and a different point. This was still the fifties, so the movie accepts, sadly but with a sense of inevitability, that freedom has limits. By the finish, Kahuna is tearing down his beach shack and taking a regular job as an airline pilot, and Moondoggie and Gidget are going back to school. The world is reaching out and claiming them, but it's not an evil world, and part of the reason they're conforming is simply because they want to. In any case, they will keep some of this freedom even as they concede to normal life.

So the utopia ends, and we feel a little sad because we know who Gidget and Moondoggie are going to be in five years and ten years and twenty years and thirty years. They're back on the moving carpet of conformity and will never get off. But we also know who they are inside, and we know that a lot of life is lived inside. They're different for this experience, and they'll stay different. They had this moment.

Easy Rider (1969) is not a movie ever mentioned alongside *Gidget*, but it deals with some of the same issues—the difficulty of freedom, the cost of it, the hard discipline of it, and the ultimate impossibility of it. Peter Fonda and Dennis Hopper are a pair of bikers who smuggle cocaine into Los Angeles and take off on a road trip, hoping to carry their California way of life safely across the country to Mardi Gras in Louisiana. But the spectacle of freedom is not congenial to the 1960s Southern mentality.

No matter what they do, people won't leave them alone. For refuge, they find pockets of community—a literal commune, at one point—and they find others who, like them, are trying to live in a state of euphoria, a life of drugs, sex, and varied, interesting experiences. But wherever the men go, violence rains down on them. A traveling companion (Jack Nicholson) is killed, and the movie ends when both protagonists are murdered.

You could say that the movie externalizes the forces that, in *Gidget*, are internalized. In *Gidget*, the people realize they can't be free. In *Easy Rider*, a malign element within the culture, repulsed and perhaps terrified by the spectacle of freedom, shows them that they are not allowed to be free—and prevents them from remaining free.

Obviously, movies are more than their messages, and the mood that *Easy Rider* evokes, very much of its time, makes the 1969 film immune to obsolescence. Its built-in obsolescence, its grounding in the era, is its whole point, and was probably its point from the first day of its release. But it is funny to consider that, in its own way, the discounted *Gidget* is more thematically complex than *Easy Rider*. Years later, *Easy Rider* seems like the product of a paranoid hippiedom, perceiving itself trapped in a world intent on blowing its buzz. Sure, it's possible that biker hippies going cross-country from L.A. to LA might meet a bad fate, but the odds were seriously against it, even in 1969. Meanwhile, the compromise that *Gidget* concludes with is poignant and universal, because, in a way, we all must come to that crossroads. Life is always a balance between freedom and conformity, between uncertainty and security.

We like to think that the desire to be free is such a hallmark of our collective American fantasy, from *Huckleberry Finn* through *Thelma and Louise*, for the simple reason that Americans love freedom and because the country's seemingly limitless space allows us to dream. But the truth is, American society is one with few safety nets, in which the dangers of failure are real and have consequences.

In fact, Americans have always been a people in search of

a dollar, in search of the freedom that comes *with* security, not the freedom that *eschews* security. We gravitate toward these other stories not because we're free but because we feel anything *but* free. We want to be at one with the beach and the horizon, and we want to skip the part where we spend thirty or forty years working to find that slice of peace. Perhaps we need both spectacles in these films—that of idyllic freedom and that of people being pulled back into the clutches of conformity. Perhaps that combination is unconsciously consoling to us.

ALTAMONT IS THE BOOKEND TO *MONTEREY POP*, the nightmare to the late sixties' utopian California dream, the end to *Monterey Pop*'s beginning. But before we get to the Altamont documentary, *Gimme Shelter* (1970), we would do well to take a detour across the country to Woodstock, and to Michael Wadleigh's 1970 documentary of the same name. It chronicles the three-day rock concert that took place in upstate New York from August 15 to 18, 1969.

The legend—or perhaps the right word is cliché—by which this history is remembered is that Woodstock represented an idyllic sixties vision, and Altamont, later that year, signaled the hell that followed. But a cold, close look at the almost four-hour *Woodstock* tells you that that dream, which began with such promise in California two years earlier, was already beginning to sour. First, the drugs were getting out of hand. To watch the Wadleigh film today is to be stunned by the incoherence of most of the people interviewed, including the performers. Some of them just sound befuddled and well-meaning, but others have clearly blown out their minds, even if only temporarily (we'll never know). In any case, the utopia is clearly beginning to take on serious casualties.

Meanwhile, the bullshit level is cranked up to eleven from the very first day. Indeed, before the festival has barely begun, the party line of the promoters and the patrons is that it's downright amazing that hundreds of thousands of people, drugged into a stupor, can manage to go three days without killing each other. That's a pretty low bar. As the concert continues, the utopian idea comes more and more into focus and more and more absurd: Perhaps Woodstock, the idea goes, could be the model for a happy, peace-loving, beautiful society?

But really? This is a model? Hundreds of thousands of intoxicated people, unable to wash, all but sitting in their own slop, cheering for a series of aristocrats that swoop down to entertain them and then leave? Meanwhile, the army flies in food and the slave classes clean out the Port-O-Sans? That's sustainable as a societal model? That's a good starting point?

By the way, unlike at Monterey Pop, there seem to be only a few women at Woodstock. Instead, the audience is pretty much wall to wall scruffy guys hoping to meet women, who, for the most part, were smart enough to stay home. It's also clear that a lot of uncool people have decided to crash the party. We see them dancing slowly and weirdly, trying to be noticed, trying to get someone, anyone, to pronounce them "far out," but no one does or ever will. It's as if everything that was spontaneous and irresistible two years earlier had solidified into a series of codified gestures that anyone could adopt—exaggerated dance moves they could master from watching the party scene on *Laugh-In* every week. Some of them obviously did.

It makes you wonder if this sixties California dream just isn't for everybody. Maybe you have to be cool. Or pure of heart. Or beautiful. Or talented. Maybe you even have to be in California. But clearly something has gone seriously wrong even by Woodstock, and yet you can't pin it on one cause, because it's a combination of things—hard drugs, commercialism, self-consciousness, phoniness, or maybe the tendency of life to regress toward the mean of grunginess, averageness, pedestrianness, unromanticness. But you just know, watching this, that reality is biting at the edge of this fantasy, and sooner or later, when everyone's looking the other way, this fantasy will be devoured altogether.

GIMME SHELTER **STARTED OUT** as a documentary of the Rolling Stones 1969 tour, which was supposed to end in triumph with a free concert in San Francisco's Golden Gate Park. The concert was later moved to the somewhat less idyllic (and less ideally located) Altamont Speedway in Tracy, California, an hour's drive inland. What ensued was a cautionary example of the consequences of self-delusion and a reminder that no one is immune, neither the cynical nor the sincere.

And so everyone descends, hundreds of thousands of people in search of a gathering-of-the-tribes communion. Trusting in some counterculture fantasy, the Rolling Stones, who are headlining this day-long event, decide against conventional security, figuring that peace and love will reign supreme. Instead, they hire, of all people, the Hells Angels, who are on drugs like the fans, but different drugs, methamphetamines. And the Angels start beating on the fans.

As the film documents, the whole first part of the concert is a terrifying catastrophe. Violence keeps breaking out. Beatings. Mick Jagger has to stop songs midway to deal with the commotion in front of him. Keith Richards starts trading words with the Hells Angels. The Stones are in a nightmare situation in which they can't leave without starting a riot. At the same time, they are in danger every minute they're on stage.

The movie takes as its climax the killing of one of the people at the concert. Eighteen-year-old Meredith Hunter makes the mistake of pulling a gun on a Hells Angel and ends up stabbed to death. The documentary, without explicitly saying so, leaves the impression that the concert ended at this point, or that, at least, it didn't go on much past that. But in fact, the concert went to full length, and after that outburst of violence the night settled down, such that people watching the show from a distance really had no idea that what they'd attended would go down in history as both the end of the 1960s and a legendary disaster.

It should be said that that show was an only-in-California experience, in that it took place on December 6. By then, Bethel, New York, the site of the Woodstock festival, was freezing cold, but California was still open for business as an endless-summer musical site. And appropriately so, in the sense that the concert itself seems an attempt to push things—the summer, the ethos, the logistics of space and population—to the limit. At the start of the concert, the movie shows some of the people, including Mick Jagger, spouting the party line about peace and about the concert as a new model for civilization. By the end, they're all just relieved to escape with their lives—back to *actual* civilization.

THE ASSOCIATION OF CALIFORNIA with utopian ideas derives, initially, from the weather, which, from the standpoint of much of the rest of the country, appears rather miraculous. In the East, you can be stewing in 95-degree heat and know with absolute certainty that within five months the weather will still be rotten, but in a completely different way. Meanwhile, it's always nice out in California, and if it isn't, you can always wait a day.

The idea of California as a utopia also derives from the sort of people who come here and the reasons for which they come. It's a place that attracts people who want to get away from everything they know, which means everything predigested in terms of thought and behavior. That includes, to some degree, all manner of established ideology. People want to be free, and they come to California to live a somewhat improvised life.

Yet there is a human tendency, in the absence of a structure, to impose a structure, to take predilections, tendencies, and interests and find within them an underlying point or ideology, a system for dealing with life. And in the absence of any overarching and dominant formula, the sky is the limit in terms of this ideology. People are free to create whatever they want and, if they are persuasive, to seek followers.

The assumption that life has a secret and that it's just a matter of discovering it and living according to it is, in itself, a form of utopian thinking. But it's also a fear reaction to freedom itself. Utopian ideology is the escape—a way to have earthly paradise and the promise of paradise both at the same time.

But because such ideologies are grounded in fear and yet present themselves as idealistic and revelatory, they can be dangerous. The fear that motivates them is concealed from the proselytizer, while it is, in fact, the driving force. And so there becomes a drive to enlist people into the cult, practice, religion, or philosophy, if only to make the world safe for those who participate.

America is a judgmental nation, and the judgment comes from the paranoia of not feeling safe, of feeling constantly threatened. In Europe a man may go for a morning run and be regarded as merely a man going for a morning run. In America, he is a moral proposition to be judged and pronounced upon. Some will think, "I should do that." Others might think, "Does he really think he's going to lose weight that way?" And still others might think, "That's not healthy—just ask Jim Fixx, except you can't, because he's dead."

Not only do we create ideology where it isn't, but we infer ideology into places where it simply is not present. A critic, for instance, might endorse a film or a play, and readers, upon finding out what the movie or play is about, might become disturbed. Even without seeing the movie or play, they will imagine an entire society and culture based on the values expressed in that movie or play. And then they will imagine—all this takes place in the blink of an eye—how they themselves might fare in such a world. Not well, obviously, and so, they panic. Thus, within seconds, they have reacted to the idea of this work of art as though it were a threat to their continued existence. And thus we get angry letters to the critic and passionate expressions of hate toward or disapproval of the people involved in that movie or play.

To the recipients of such blasts of anger and panic, these reactions will seem absurdly outsized, but only if the recipients fail to realize that their respective correspondents have determined that this or that work of art is out to kill them.

The ideology-free nature of California makes it a breeding ground for new bad ideologies and their concomitant utopian visions. Thus, long before the 1960s, long before the evangelist Aimee Semple McPherson started preaching over a hundred years ago in San Diego, California was known as a beacon for faith healers, spiritualists, quacks, nudists, and miracle cures. Just as artists made a beeline for Paris, if you were a charismatic nut and wanted to start a cult, you went to California—that's where people were bound to be receptive.

Because California was a land of free thinkers, a Californian, even in distress, might regard as a defeat the adoption of some familiar and organized system of comfort—that is, organized religion. At the same time, a brand new ideology pointing to a bright utopia might present itself to the same mind as of a piece with his or her sense of forward motion, of being an emblem of freedom, not mental confinement, even when this ideology takes on the contours of a cult, as in the Paul Thomas Anderson movie *The Master* (2012). Then, once you're inside the circle, everyone outside of it is unenlightened. And the more esoteric and enclosed the ideology is, the more prone it is to paranoia and even violence.

It must be acknowledged that lethal ideologies are not the sole province of California or, for that matter, the United States. With reference to California, I'm talking about something more specific, something that presents itself as benign and peaceful, as embodying love. Hitler, Mao, Mussolini—they knew they were not calling for universal love, and so did their followers. But it's hard to imagine Charles Manson or Jim Jones selling their particular brands of utopian psychosis outside of California. This is the place where hell begins as a great idea on a gorgeous sunny day.

OF ALL THE UTOPIAN IDEOLOGIES, the most pervasive is the indefinable yet unmistakable one that's sold to us through movies. The movies package stars as idealized versions of average people, as platonic ideals of certain looks and values. And as viewers identify with these personalities and feel vicarious glory in the glorification of others, they start to imagine the movies themselves as the possible vehicle for their own transfiguration, their own elevation into some ideal state.

Basically, movie stars are like patron saints or avatars of audience self-love, and often the act of basking in them and loving them is a form of praying to oneself. It stands to reason, then, that both supremely confident people and supremely insecure people should intuit this reality and want to experience the devotion themselves. The first type knows they deserve it. The other type knows they need it.

The Day of the Locust (1975), John Schlesinger's film based on the Nathanael West novel, is forceful in showing us both the utopian mirage and its reality—it's like getting Monterey Pop and Altamont in the same movie. William Atherton played a young artist who arrives in Southern California, and we see it through his eyes. It's simply beautiful—all those mansions built in the 1920s. All that vegetation that makes it look like Tuscany, only without the green-blue sky that Tuscany has. This is the bright-blue California sky.

The artist is named Tod Hackett, probably because he's bound to end up a hack, like most people in Hollywood. But at this stage, all is well. He meets a young woman, Faye (Karen Black), and becomes attracted to her. She seems like the embodiment, the living expression, of everything the place promises—youth, sex, freshness, gratification of all one's hopes and senses. And in one sense, he's right. She *is* the embodiment of Hollywood, just not in a good way.

She is beautiful, but has no talent, so her career can't go anywhere. This lack of talent seems related to a lack of values, or lack of some essential authenticity. Indeed, every time she is tempted by authenticity—for example, the possibility of having a relationship with Tod, whom she flirts with—she rejects it. She tells him she can't allow herself to fall in love with a man without money.

At one point, she becomes a call girl, and the expectation, based on a thousand previous movies, is that this will be devastating to her. But no, she doesn't have the typical nature or morals to be bothered by this. She's unfazed. This is Hollywood and the usual moral constraints don't apply.

There's a scene in which Hackett witnesses the collapse of a movie set. In what seems almost comical to think about (though it's not intended for laughs in the film), the Napoleonic Wars are being shot inside the studio, and so a hill has been rigged with earth and shrubs on top of a scaffolding. The scaffolding caves in, injuring dozens of extras, and though it's made clear that the dangers were anticipated, it's suggested that no one will be held responsible.

That scene prefigures the ending. The notion of a world of illusion, papered over an abyss and about to drop into disaster, finds its fruition in the climactic scene in which the war movie opens at a theater called "Mr. Khan's Pleasure Dome." A grand premiere is the ultimate in presenting movie stars as royalty, and aside from the Oscars, it's the clichéd fantasy for everyone who aspires to movie stardom—to be on the red carpet, to be glamorous, to be on the inside of the rope line, to be able to go inside the pleasure dome instead of having to stay outside, forever.

But it's only for so long that people can be expected to live on dreams and on the vicarious thrill of others living the life they wish they had. And so, one person snaps and commits a bizarre act of violence, and the admiring crowd becomes a mob. Curiously, the crowd doesn't turn on the royalty in their midst but rather, as is so often the case in real life, it turns on itself. And what we witness is a spectacle of repressed disappointment, disillusionment, and dissatisfaction exploding out into the open. All of these feelings that can't be said out loud, that can't be admitted for fear of being revealed to oneself as a loser, are suddenly out there and rampaging.

This is the consequence of promising people that which can't be delivered, of telling them that a world exists that they can plainly see does not. The pleasure dome is not for them, and the promised utopia was a con job all along.

EPILOGUE

Any book about California in the movies inevitably must become, to some degree, a tale of two cities. California, in reality, is much more than Los Angeles and San Francisco, but the California we find onscreen is very often one or the other. Every so often you do see a movie that expresses another California location with vividness, and those are to be treasured—for example, *Fat City* (1972), the John Huston film based on the Leonard Gardner novel about two boxers, one younger (Jeff Bridges), one a little older (Stacy Keach).

Fat City depicts a down-at-the-heels Skid Row version of Stockton that doesn't exist anymore, but the notable thing about the film—aside from the authentic locations—is that everybody is nice to each other. Watching it, we keep expecting the characters to clash in some dire conflict, but the drama doesn't come from there but rather from the characters' individual struggles to survive hard times and have a life of dignity. There's none of the barbed or hidden or twisted atmosphere of the big cities. Everybody is decent, sincere, and okay—no hidden agenda, no attitude.

In a different but not entirely dissimilar way, we can appreciate writer-director Greta Gerwig's expressive use of Sacramento in *Lady Bird* (2017), with its teenage protagonist who longs to live in a "real" place, with real culture. Meanwhile, the audience sees a town that looks not only entirely real but nice, a place with room for a teenager to grow up and grow in confidence, a place in which to have a life, and to launch a life.

Among recent films, the most promising development is the emergence of Oakland as a location with a distinct filmmaking personality, as we see in the 2018 films *Sorry to Bother You*, directed by Boots Riley, and in *Blindspotting*, directed by Carlos López Estrada and written by its lead stars, Daveed Diggs and Rafael Casal. Both depict a place of extreme tension, where anything can go wrong at any time.

Riley's film, which has surreal and science fiction elements, is charged with anxiety, and it's almost as if a reaction to the anxiety propels the movie's innovation. For example, when its protagonist, a telemarketer, calls someone, he and his desk come crashing through that person's roof. In a comical and immediately accessible image, the movie communicates both the inconvenience of the call, from the standpoint of the person receiving it, and the embarrassment of the person who has to make it.

Though very different from each other, both *Sorry to Bother You* and *Blindspotting* adopt a tone that allows for a range spanning from tense drama to absurdist comedy. That seeming disharmony is resolved by those films being tied to a specific place that not only contains but also makes sense of these elements.

Blindspotting is more explicitly about Oakland specifically, not just about modern America generally. It begins beautiful, with a series of shots showing various aspects of city life—the skateboarders, the BART train, a Whole Foods store, and kids playing jump rope. Underscoring these scenes isn't hip hop music, which might have been the obvious go-to, but the drinking song from Verdi's *La Traviata*. The point is that this is a grand place of grand human emotion. The life here isn't a subset of life. This isn't a subculture. This is specific and universal and today's California.

Once again, it is a curious thing to see how often, over the course of film history, some of the greatest films have been topical, either in their subject matter or in the ideas they espouse. Movies such as *Sorry to Bother You* and *Blindspotting* show that the California movie is always growing and innovating.

One area in which there is considerable room for innovation is the representation of Latinx people in American film, generally. A 2019 study by the Annenberg Inclusion Initiative found that of the top one hundred movies in each of the previous twelve years, only 3 percent of the lead characters and 4.5 percent of all characters were Latinx. This imbalance is especially bizarre when we consider that Latinx people make up 19 percent of the American population.

One has to wonder if this is the result of some collective failure of the imagination, or of the box office, or both, or if there is some other reason. In any case, what makes this dearth mysterious is that a few decades ago there was a series of superb Latinx films, among them *Zoot Suit* (1981), *La Bamba* (1987), *Stand and Deliver* (1988), and *Mi Familia* (1995), which seemed to signal the dawn of a new era. But of these films, only *La Bamba* was a certified box-office smash, and *Mi Familia*—a near-great family epic—grossed only $11 million. That disappointment might have ended, for a generation, that small, promising burst of creativity.

Yet nothing seems more inevitable than the increased representation of Latinx experiences in twenty-first century American cinema. Assuming this comes about in the usual way, Hollywood won't be motivated by any sense of altruism or social concern, but out of some belated, irrefutable discovery of a lucrative market. In other words, someone will make a movie that unlocks the box-office power of Latinx stories, and the floodgates of art and commerce will open—perhaps never to close again. And California will almost certainly be at the center of all of it.

This is how it has been and how it should be. In its ideas, in its vision of America, in its artistic response to the world, the California movie invariably stakes out a place in the near future and then shows the rest of the country how to get there.

THERE CAN BE LITTLE DOUBT that the world has been transformed by California and the values it exports. To a large extent, we should celebrate this, even as we notice that wherever we travel, people are taking pictures of themselves and their food.

Egocentrism has always been a human failing, but Hollywood put it on a fast track in the twentieth century, a state of affairs that technology has exacerbated in the new millennium. Today, egocentrism is an epidemic, and yet seeing it all around us should make us humble. Here's why: In olden days, people loved themselves in secret, believing themselves to be worthy and special—better than other people. But such was their discretion that we had no idea they thought of themselves so highly. Now, with egocentrism and narcissism out of the closet and galloping through our culture, we are constantly forced to see people who really shouldn't love themselves at all and yet love themselves ardently, fervently, and sincerely—yes, even as much as we love *our*selves. This is outrageous, ludicrous, and unthinkable, but even worse, it's unsettling, because it inevitably must make us examine our own preferences. The sight of all these preening people makes us face the possibility that we, too, have been operating out of a delusional bias. It makes us see that our own self-love, which we'd always thought was grounded in discernment of merit, was really based on proximity.

Oh, yes, and have you seen people *posing* for pictures lately? Not too long ago, people used to be uncomfortable just standing there getting their picture taken. They used to be embarrassed to pose in front of the picture taker, much less under the gaze of everyone else lining up in front of the Eiffel Tower. But today, people immediately assume the pose and the vacant smile of a fashion model. The second after the picture is taken, they resume their normal personalities in a way that bespeaks a change in custom, not of consciousness. But the photo itself is no longer a private token but a means of promoting a vision of one's life to the world—and, by the world's reflection, showing it back to the self.

This makes everyone their own little movie star, and I must say it makes me feel a little like a Roman Catholic in the days when the Protestant Reformation was just taking hold. After all, in the old religion of a generation ago, people worshipped in the Church of Self through the proxies of saints in the form of movie stars. Now, the devoted have eliminated the need for the intercession of various middlemen and have taken to worshipping the great god of Self directly.

Where does this all lead? Probably to nowhere bad. Human nature has a way of staying intrinsically the same through all kinds of fads and cultural tribulations—social, technological, and otherwise. But however this plays out, this modern-day preoccupation with the self does seem in a line of succession from the California ideal as expressed through movies, and it should caution us as we extol, not without reason, the influence—indeed the triumph—of the California ideal throughout the world.

Point being, we can love individuality, independent thought, creativity, freedom, nonconformism, material comfort, and youthful splendor, even as we recognize that it's possible to overdose on the most useful and necessary medicine. There's a dark end of the spectrum—solipsism, selfishness, spiritual emptiness, and impenetrable loneliness—and we don't want that nightmare: Seven and a half billion people with selfie sticks shrieking, "Me, me, me!" in a vacuum, unheard by anyone.

ACKNOWLEDGMENTS

The people that must be acknowledged first are those to whom the book is dedicated. Bob Graham (1938–2019) was my first editor at the *San Francisco Chronicle*. He was one of the people that hired me; otherwise, I never would have moved to California from the East Coast. He mentored me daily, going over every single word I wrote for my first eighteen months on the job. He didn't necessarily teach me everything *he* knew about journalism, but he definitely taught me everything *I* know.

Jennifer Hengen was my first agent and is responsible for my becoming somebody who is able to get a book published. For my first book, she stuck with me through eight variations of the same proposal—and eighty rejections—until we finally got a yes. It took almost four years. Like Bob, she believed in me before there was any reason to, and before anyone else did.

So without Bob there would have been, for me, no California, and without Jennifer there would have been no books.

As for *Dream State*, in particular, I am indebted to Steve Wasserman, the publisher of Heyday, for both suggesting the topic and for letting me run with it. He also came up with the book's title. I had something else—you wouldn't have liked it as much.

Emmerich Anklam, assistant to the publisher at Heyday, read the initial draft and made suggestions that were invaluable. Gayle Wattawa, Heyday's editorial director, managed the editing process with taste, intelligence, and sensitivity, and Lisa Marietta executed a line edit with a care and focus that resulted in some important additions and clarifications.

My wife, Amy Freed, was very helpful during the writing process, even more than usual. She remained enthusiastic about this project from start to finish and provided lots of ideas that I've happily included under my own name, because California is, after all, a community property state.

Finally, I feel an imprecise and yet distinct desire to thank California itself—the people for welcoming me, the artists who distilled and implanted the California idea into the world's consciousness, and even the politicians, for making California a remarkably livable, beautiful, and humane place ... at least most of the time.

INDEX

ABOUT THE AUTHOR

Mick LaSalle is the film critic for the *San Francisco Chronicle*. He is the author of three previous books: *Complicated Women: Sex and Power in Pre-Code Hollywood*, a history and critical study of the actresses who worked during the pre-censorship era of 1929–1934; *Dangerous Men: Pre-Code Hollywood and the Birth of the Modern Man*; and *The Beauty of the Real: What Hollywood Can Learn from Contemporary French Actresses*. LaSalle lives in San Francisco, California.